Born in 1948 in Bois-Colombes, **Catherine Millet** is an art critic, curator and founder of the prestigious magazine *Art Press*. Her 2002 memoir *The Sexual Life of Catherine M.* was translated into forty languages and has sold over five million copies, 250,000 in the UK alone. In 2005, she published the monograph *Dalí et Moi* (*Dalí and Me*). *Jealousy* (*Jour de Souffrance*) was published to critical acclaim in France in 2008 and spent many weeks on the bestseller list. Catherine Millet lives in Paris with the poet and novelist Jacques Henric.

The Sexual Life of Catherine M.

'This is the most explicit book about sex ever written by a woman, though it is far from pornographic. Catherine Millet sets about coolly and rationally exploring her insatiable appetites… and she has lived to tell a tale that is the opposite of lurid. It is a comprehensive and elegant performance' Edmund White

'It is Millet's subversive achievement to describe pleasure for its own sake' *New Statesman*

'Millet is a woman who writes plainly; who tells the truth about desire' *Guardian*

'Graceful, thoughtful, oddly charming, and profoundly pornographic. A bold, intelligent, pioneering tour de force' *Kirkus Reviews*

jealousy

catherine millet

translated by helen stevenson

A complete catalogue record for this book can be obtained
from the British Library on request

The right of Catherine Millet to be identified as the author of
this work has been asserted by her in accordance with the
Copyright, Designs and Patents Act 1988

First published as *Jour de Souffrance* in 2008 by
Flammarion SA, Paris

First published in this translation in 2009 by Serpent's Tail,
an imprint of Profile Books Ltd
3A Exmouth House
Pine Street
London EC1R 0JH
website: www.serpentstail.com

ISBN 978 1 84668 718 1

Designed and typeset by Sue Lamble
Printed by Clays, Bungay, Suffolk

10 9 8 7 6 5 4 3 2 1

FSC
Mixed Sources
Product group from well-managed
forests and other controlled sources
Cert no. SGS-COC-2061
www.fsc.org
© 1996 Forest Stewardship Council

The paper this book is printed on
is certified by the © 1996 Forest
Stewardship Council A.C. (FSC).
It is ancient-forest friendly.
The printer holds FSC chain of
custody SGS-COC-2061

summary

Unless one believes in predestination, it is clear that the circumstances of any encounter with another person, which, for the sake of ease, we attribute to chance, are in fact the result of an incalculable series of decisions taken at each crossroad in life, which secretly steer us towards them. Even the most important of these encounters may not have been consciously sought, or even desired. Rather, each of us proceeds like an artist or writer, who constructs a piece of work through a succession of choices; a gesture or word does not inevitably determine the gesture or word which follows, but instead confronts the author with a new choice. A painter who has used a touch of red may choose to mute it by juxtaposing a touch of violet; he may choose to make it sing with a touch of green. In the long run, whatever mental image of the painting he may have started out with, the sum of all the decisions he takes, some of them unforeseen, will give a different result. Thus we lead our lives by a series of acts which are in fact far more considered than we care to admit – since to take full and clear responsibility for them would be a great burden – but which nevertheless set us on the path of people we have unknowingly been gravitating towards for some time.

How did Jacques' face first register on my field of vision? I could not say. Elsewhere I have written that I was struck by his voice, as heard twice removed by a tape machine (it was a recording) and the telephone (down which someone played the recording to me). On the other hand, there is no visual image lodged in my memory signaling his epiphany in my life. A curious fact, since I am blessed with an excellent visual memory but have no ear at all. Perhaps it is precisely because my ear is relatively little used that I have managed to isolate one of the rare occasions on which it was sensitive, whereas my eye is so much in use and so ready to observe details, at times, it seems, indiscriminately, that I sometimes feel like one of those mad people who are unable to sift and order the visual signals which reach them from the outside world. Thus my first image relating to Jacques is a *Gestalt*, his presence as a dark, dense mass, inseparable from the surrounding space, which was lighter, white or rather cream coloured, its depth – I remember this quite clearly – delineated by a board fixed to the wall, serving as a work surface, and the door which led to the toilet.

I should say that we were having to concentrate on a page in a catalogue where there was a piece of text he'd written, which we had to correct by hand. We had been working for several hours, sitting side by side in the narrow office. I can still see the page, the text printed in characters imitating those of a typewriter. I can also see the house of the friend where he took me to dinner once the tedious job was done, and the bed, doubling as a sofa, on which we sat chatting after the meal; I can even still make out the faces of one or two of the other guests. But what marks out Jacques at that moment is still not his image, but a very discreet gesture, in which he just brushed my wrist with the back of his index finger. The circumstances of this memory enable me to identify a phenomenon I have observed at the moment when sensual pleasure first starts to stir; my visual attention seems to focus less on the actual object of my desire than on what surrounds it. In fact it is a reflex we all have in public, to put people off the scent. It affords the twofold pleasure of contact and dissimulation: we gaze intently into the eyes of the person on our right, to distract attention from the person on our left, who is stroking our knee under the table. But could it not be, also, that we respond generously to the blossoming of one of our senses, so that, in this instance, even as my skin was enjoying the touch of a man's hand, softer than any I had ever known, or ever would know, my eyes could focus all their curiosity on his friends?

The image appears slowly in the developing tray of memories. I can recall, without hesitation, the position of our bodies in his bed the following morning, while, as often happens at such times, a voluble exposition of our selves as social beings succeeded the hasty exposition of our physical selves, and although I can still judge the exact level of daylight in the room during this exchange, it is only in memories from a later date that I begin to see the outline of his face and fill in the details of his features.

Significantly, in these memories, which belong to a period when our relationship was already established and steady, the image is not a close-up, which might have shown his face, with the expression in his eyes or mouth, but, at first, an establishing shot: for example, I see him parking his motorbike on the pavement opposite, and track him as he crosses the street, detaches his body from the rolling stream of other passers-by and comes towards the terrace of the café where a group – myself among them – is waiting for him. It seems to me that it is now that I notice the slightly elongated rectangle, the regularity of his head, accentuated by his short-cropped hair, which is already beginning to thin at the crown. This geometry is echoed in the square-set torso – the shoulders, waist and sides seem all to be of equal measure – accentuated by the loose- fitting shirt. In other words, I could only register his features by taking time and – literally – a step backwards, in imitation of certain painters who work in the old-fashioned manner, taking several steps backwards to get a better sense of their subject, the relation, proportionally, to the setting, and the effect of contrast with it.

I did not have a laser, instead of eyes, with which to pierce the world's haze and immediately cut out the face of Jacques Henric. Although I had retained the childhood habit of drifting off into daydreams, my imagination respected its boundaries and I never imported into my life the ideal image of a man, formed in my imagination and projected onto the features of every man I met. I was twenty-four; I had been born in the Paris suburbs, in an unpromising environment, which I left aged eighteen, my only baggage the books I'd read. I needed, therefore, to widen my experience of the real world, and I yearned to discover new worlds, just as others at that time were taking to the open road, their rucksacks on their backs. The backpackers did not settle somewhere straight away. Similarly, it was not until my eye had 'photographed' a wide variety of groups that I felt the desire to draw a ring

around one face in particular. Romantic clichés were not my
thing then; they still aren't today and I could never say that I
recognized Jacques as one in a thousand; no, it was rather that
until I'd met a thousand others I could not know that at the
root of my relationship with him was a feeling whose nature
and durability distinguished it from all others. Just as when
faced with an intriguing, but apparently banal painting, which
conceals an anamorphosis, you try to discover the precise angle
from which, out of disparate elements, the laws of optics will
enable you to perceive an astonishing coherent object, so at
first I had to find my bearings in life, and then, having gleaned
various different impressions of a man, in circumstances which
did not particularly distinguish him from the others, put them
all together to find standing before me the one who would
move me more than any other.

From Jacques, the understated gesture of a caress with the
back of his finger. From my side I recall no one particular decisive move. After the dinner I went back home with him. Did
he need to be any more explicit for me to feel I was invited?
I'm not sure he did. That was how I lived at that time. I
remember nothing of the journey from the friend's house
where we had had dinner to the studio where he lived. Are
travellers always interested in the middle of their journey? As
I attempt, in these opening pages, to recall the circumstances
of my meeting with the man whose life I share, it is the starting
point, all those years ago, which comes back to me. The explo-
sive fuse from which my going home with Jacques that night
was the distant echo: a race across a garden. The circumstances
were these.

I was an adolescent. As I have said, I loved reading, but I
was very bad at maths and I was made to take private lessons

at the house of another girl, a friend who had similar difficulties. It so happened that the young man who taught us wrote
poetry, and had even founded a little journal with a group of
friends. The day of the last lesson came and we said goodbye
at the door of the house where my friend's family lived. I
suspect my memory has exaggerated the amount of time it
took him to walk down the garden path to the gate, because I
still have the sense to this day that at that moment I entered
upon the first big dilemma of my life. A dilemma dilates time.
It is a torture which slowly, painfully, extracts contradictory
arguments from the mind and examines them, returning now
to this one, now to the other, in order to reinforce them. For
the first time I was about to be able to tell someone who
would understand the vital significance of the statement, that
I was also a writer; the force of the words rose up within me,
I had to release them, the reflex as imperious as if, having held
my breath for too long, I had had to start breathing again. I
was gullible, convinced that one's future could be determined,
as I had read and had perhaps been taught, by a chance but
decisive meeting with an older person, by some prophetic
utterance they might make; I had in mind the kind of mythical
tale whose rhetorical devices and perennial role in literature
would be brought to my attention much later by that learned
and delightful work *The Image of the Artist*, by Ernst Kris and
Otto Kurz... But at the same time, pubescent shame held me
back. I would be making a fool of myself in front of the boy
and my friend. They would both think that I had invented this
ruse so as to keep in contact with him: as well as being good
at maths and a poet, he was very handsome. Such was preju-
dice, people would assume my motivation came more from a
desire to go out with him than from a love of literature. Or,

worse still, they would think I was one of those love-sick schoolgirls who think it cool to Write Poetry. Of course, I knew myself that my literary tastes had existed long before I met him, and that what I wrote was in no way connected with him, but I probably already had some sort of subliminal self-knowledge (acquired at a very young age by one who aspires to write – and perhaps even predating the aspiration – placing her from the very outset in the role of witness to the world and to herself) which told me that, even so, the suspicion was not entirely ill-founded. My determination to use books and works of art to gain access to a way of life other than the one offered by my upbringing went very deep, but I already had sufficient insight to realise that the charms of the maths tutor pandered imperceptibly to that determination. At least, that was how it seemed to me, at an age at which one prizes the purity of one's desires.

But it is also an age at which we still have a dream of the future, a dream based on the miraculous possibilities our imagination lays in store, before life teaches us that it can be steered down paths which are less idealized but more plentiful and diverse. It seemed impossible that such an extraordinary chance would come again. As he placed his hand on the handle of the iron gate I called out and went running over to him.

And so it came to pass. I asked if I could see him again, to give him some things to read. He fixed a date. His manner was attentive and unsurprised. I interpreted this as a slight weariness, as though he had known what I was going to do all along and his kindly air concealed a reproach for my having wasted his time a little by my hesitation. I went back to my friend, who did not seem surprised either, and asked no questions. Thus, in a very short space of time, after an intense inner struggle, I had apparently taken the most important decision of my life and no one batted an eyelid. Had they not noticed? Or was it because they had so often heard me trying to sound interesting, expressing unusual or absurd ideas, or because I had a habit of embellishing stories, they had already categorized me as an eccentric, a sort of half-way house between the family world and that of artists? I was intrigued by this failure to react. It fuelled my inevitable questioning of my future place in society, which I tried vaguely to envisage, along with the reaction it would provoke in other people.

Some writers, whether of fiction or non-fiction, may have been attracted to the activity by a pure love of books. I am not one of them. For me, the love of books has never been an absolute. It is mingled with the desire to live in a different world to that of my earliest youth, in which the only extension outwards was that of the dining room table, the leaf added for my first communion, and that of my brother, as well as for New Year's day get-togethers and some birthdays – with conversation appropriate to the occasion orbiting around it. I would be the last person to scoff at the cliché: literature as escapism. The rue Philippe-de-Metz in Bois-Colombes, where I was born, and where I spent my childhood and teenage years, was unusual in design, like a rectangular fortress in the middle of an estate of suburban villas. It was short and narrow, and composed of high, solid brick buildings, each of them virtually identical. Luckily, the second apartment we lived in was on the top floor – the seventh – and I would read by a window which gave onto a courtyard, but had nothing overlooking it. In order to escape to other lands, other times, the reader must be able to adopt the mobility of the heroes, and sometimes that of the authors themselves. The signals I received from the artistic and literary world, up on my seventh floor, came via *Readers' Digest* and *Paris Match*, and one of the contemporary models I had access to was Françoise Sagan, who was young and famous, like her characters, drove sports cars, and whom I had once seen in an interview on television explaining how to conceal a yawn at a smart party by taking a slug of whisky or a drag on a cigarette.

I never went out with the poet, who gave maths lessons because, it turned out, he was married and had a small daughter. But I did see him a few more times; we met in a café and, always in the same attentive, but slightly distant manner, he would comment favourably on what I had given him to read, and make small suggestions, or comments. One day, when he couldn't come, or it suited him not to be able to come, he sent a friend to make his apologies. Possibly the second important decision of my life was to accept the friend's invitation, but this time without any sense of the possible consequences which would follow. His friend wasn't good-looking, and he wasn't a poet, but he was single. Of the group of friends who ran the poetry journal he was the one least constrained by university or family ties, and he was financially independent; he was an enterprising young man, and his role in the group was to deliver copies to bookshops and collect the money from sales. When they decided to expand the activity of the journal by opening an art gallery, Claude was naturally found to be the person most available and qualified to run it. The journal failed, while the gallery thrived. It was in this gallery that I spent those hours correcting the catalogue along with Jacques. I had been living with Claude for four and a half years.

The picture album in our memory follows a system of classification in which the order, the corrections and the repetitions are often surprising, challenging the accepted version we have of our life. My memory of the outline of Claude, the first time I saw him, is considerably more precise than the one I have of Jacques. His stance is rather stiff, solemn almost, and although he has his back to the light I can see his expression as he introduces himself: 'You don't know me, I'm a friend of Patrick, he…' He gives me an appraising look. He sees me in bright daylight, a golden light, as it is springtime, which shines through the glass pane which goes from ceiling to floor of the half-landing. Claude has a car, if he feels like it he can decide to drive all night to the sea. It was during an escapade of this sort that I lost my virginity. Throughout the early years we spent together, Claude did a lot of driving: we would go see the Venice Biennale, Documenta in Cassel, and Prospect in Dusseldorf. There were exhibitions all over Europe: in Berlin, Cologne, Rome, Turin, Naples, we would head off to shows at the Wide White Space Gallery in Antwerp, or at Konrad Fischer in Dusseldorf. In 1972, Claude opened a second gallery in Milan, where I often went with him because I was working on the magazine *Flash Art*, whose director was one of the friend–lovers with whom I began a long-term relationship during that period. Just as I loved living between two cities, I loved going from one man to another.

The third decision was an act of long-term commitment, even if at the time it was made on the spur of the moment, as a reflex response to a challenge. Like a little shell which floats to the surface when the depths which have long lain motionless are suddenly disturbed, it was a small and insignificant remark, the kind you make without thinking, but only once a great deal of inhibition has been overcome, the kind which relates to a prosaic and everyday detail, but which will change the course of your life. I began living with Claude before even bothering to take my *bac*. The moral autonomy immediately conferred by one's first sexual relationship, together with my forays into a way of life which, I discovered, you could make up as you went along, had distracted me, both *de facto* and in practice, from the discipline of school and family.

Inevitably, my mother expressed concern about my chosen means of making a living. One day when I had dropped in at the rue Philippe de Metz to pick up some Tupperware or perhaps some clean laundry, I replied spontaneously, without even having thought about it before, and simply because I thought it would satisfy her at that moment, that I intended to write freelance articles on art for magazines. She pretended to believe me. I knew myself that I could never earn enough money doing that, but even so, unexpectedly, I found myself committed by this reply, carried away by my own boldness. For the first time, I had mentioned my desire to write to someone outside the circle of idealistic young people publishing a journal of intimate poetry, and I was even exceeding the boundaries of intimacy by seeking to satisfy this desire out in the world: it would be my job. What had been intended only as a remark to put my mother's mind at rest, and let her daughter off the hook in her impatience to get back to her young lover, gave substance to a desire possibly more urgent than that propelling her towards that lover, but which had remained buried, being so much more enigmatic and difficult to explain. Years earlier, I had copied out these words of comfort, written by Balzac: 'Nothing forges the character so much as a secret hidden at the heart of a family.' My secret was none other than these notebooks, in which I wrote down quotations, poems of my own, openings for novels. From this point on, writing would cease to be a secret, almost shameful activity, and would be openly acknowledged; it would not merely be normal, but interesting, original. Whenever someone asked me what I did I could say: 'Art criticism'. That would surprise them, I'd be left in peace.

When the gallery opened Claude went to introduce himself to the editorial team of *Les Lettres Françaises*, run by Louis Aragon, and he had become friends with a few of the people who worked on it, including Georges Boudaille, who was in charge of the 'art' pages. It was to him that I took my first ever review of an exhibition. Editors like beginners, to whom they can give little jobs that real journalists don't want any more, but who are also on the lookout for new subjects. That is how I found myself writing for *Lettres Françaises* as well as a number of other magazines which started up at that time, as a specialist in conceptual art, which involved the kind of intellectual speculation I enjoyed. For a few years, Claude shared this interest, and the copy I was correcting with Jacques was for the catalogue of the first exhibition of conceptual art ever shown in Paris.

I was too immature, of course, to appreciate that my intuition, the day of my dramatic hesitation before the attractive teacher–poet, was actually well-founded. Our internal means of transport, which convey our intellectual and sexual passions, travel along tracks which may touch, and are permeable. Not always, but often. If I had been able to step back a few years, I might have realized that my dream-world was already imbued with this mix.

During the holidays, my mother, who did not drive, often signed us up for coach trips. It was during one of these that we arrived, one evening, in one of those picturesque villages which have been transformed into stage sets for the 'artistic life', to appeal to tourists, who will then purchase ceramics of dubious taste. We went into a café. At the back of the vaulted room, a group of young people sat listening, while one of them played the guitar; there was a girl in the group. Naively, I saw in her a young bohemian who lived in the village, about to spend an evening, perhaps even the night, listening to music, singing, entering a pocket of time without constraints, while I would be getting back on the bus. As I watched them, the idea came to me that one of them would notice me and, from some kind of sign on my face, would realise that I belonged, by virtue of my aspirations, with them. What do you pin your hopes on when your family circle has no social connections, and could not even begin to imagine any means of helping you realize your intellectual or artistic ambitions – quite simply because they are unaware of the existence of certain activities, certain ways of living, not to mention making a living – and you yourself are still too much within that circle to know yourself what steps you might take, and are still far from being able to produce anything concrete which might justify such steps? You dream, you wait for the mythical meeting at the crossroads. In my case, the culture from which the models for my fantasies were drawn was that of romance. I could imagine no other way of escaping from my suburban world than one involving, perhaps, a providential stranger who would notice me on the concourse of the Gare St-Lazare and would pluck me from the slumbering crowd. The idea was not fully formed, but it was clear that because I was a woman, my salvation would come from a man who would, of course, discover my aspirations, my talents (of which I was quite confident!), but would pick me out, in the first instance, on the basis of my face.

I had kept my thoughts about the group to myself, but my mother must have noticed my interest in them. As we were leaving the café she opined forcefully that the girl probably 'slept around'. Several times, during my childhood, I heard my mother use the word 'whore' of a film actress or any other woman who flaunted herself, and each time what shocked me was not the vulgarity of the word but the sudden nature of the outburst, when no one had even asked for her opinion of the woman in question, as well as the tone of hatred in which she spoke. At such times I felt ashamed of my mother, as though she was the one who had behaved indecently.

There was no room in my daydreams for the most likely scenario, which was the one which actually came about, in which there would be two of us, leaving the same small town somewhere out on the line from the Gare St Lazare, that we would help one another on the journey, and go through our sentimental and professional education together. For the one respect in which it did follow the pattern of the original story was in the close conjunction of social emancipation – the ways Claude and I found of thinking and working outside the conventional norms – and sexual liberation.

We had sex together, we had sex together with other people, and each of us with other people separately. Once this pattern had been established, it was never made official. What

I mean by this is that we never made any kind of verbal contract, and just as we never actually decided to become a couple, we never bothered, either, to define individual actions which our situation disallowed, even once we had discovered through painful experience that at particular moments, which lay beyond our control, it was necessary to have what we did not quite dare call taboos. The alternative was unbearable. As far as I remember, no great declarations of love passed between myself and Claude before I moved into the little apartment where there were certainly two chairs, but as yet no table, nor did we spend much time discussing how I was going to contribute to the rent. Similarly, over the next few years, when the punching and the weeping set in, once an incident was over, we never chose to comment either on the incident itself or on its occasionally violent nature. I am not even sure the word 'jealousy' ever crossed our minds.

Certain situations, namely those which we each experienced differently, were unbearable. For instance, Claude might be aware that I was off on a trip and would be joining a male friend. I might happen to come home a day later than arranged. At that point, he would start to suffer, but say nothing. Perhaps he had been suffering before that and simply felt authorized by the delay to express it, perhaps not. Whether it was caused by his unconscious resistance to our freedom, or by some genuine wrong I had committed by returning late, or by something else altogether, I had abused a contract, the terms of which had never been agreed. Freedom was meant to be the rule, but we had never defined the limits of that freedom, either explicitly or tacitly. As a result, the reasons for Claude's suffering were never made clear. The only way he could show it was by attacking me physically, coldly, almost deliberately; I never saw any anger in his face. His expression was one of concentration, as he judged his punches to the nearest millimetre, according to what was perhaps a sort of internal conversion table from emotional to bodily pain. So, it seemed to me that there was nothing I could do to fix the rule I was supposed to have broken and which had, in any case, been arbitrarily imposed by him. When it came down to it, these scenes in which we each used words and gestures which should have been utterly unacceptable were as free of consequences as if we had suddenly just stopped, in obedience to the voice of a director shouting 'Cut!' – and they never influenced my subsequent behaviour in any way.

For my own part, I was aware on at least two occasions of a violent desire on Claude's part for another woman. The weeping and recrimination this provoked in me were never the expression of a fear that our own relationship might be at risk. Here again, his behaviour remained a mystery to me, especially when his desire was frustrated. I was amazed to find him so fragile, he was normally so self-assured, even if his pain was expressed in a paradoxical way, so that he became even more silent than usual. I watched him with incredulity, in the same way I might have watched a display of witchcraft. Not only did I not know the rules, but in any case, the show was not intended for me. Regardless of whether the object of Claude's desire was myself or another person, I found I was unable to interpret his behaviour and it just looked to me like a 'drive for possession', one of those emotions which are forged in infancy, but may long outlive it, and which continue to determine the behaviour of many young adults. Indeed, they provided the framework of my own psychology. What I was trying to communicate through my own outbursts and fits of hysteria, during which my body undoubtedly became a battlefield for feelings which I could not adequately put into words, was an essentially narcissistic sense of frustration.

Each time, Claude became interested in particularly pretty girls. Now I was so intoxicated by sexual freedom I had come to think of my body as having unlimited sexual potential, I was certain that I could exploit all its resources in all sorts of different situations, with as many different partners as came my way. If I had ever stopped to think that this certainty was not something I could take for granted, I might have likened my experience to something I had seen done by certain free jazz pianists, Cecil Taylor, or Sun Ra, who were not content simply to play on the strings of their instruments, but also got sounds from the wood, played them in conjunction with unusual objects, or invited the audience to join in… This body of mine might never come up against the limits which confined the other aspects of my person. In the short term, it compensated for my shyness in social situations and stood in for an intellectual purpose which was still rather vague. Although of course I never actually expressed it to myself like this, I must have credited my body with a kind of omnipotence, and been afflicted with a kind of megalomania which exclusively affected the way I thought about my body. Added to this was the fact that my freedom ushered me into an arena into which other women rarely ventured, particularly women of my age, and as a result I was able to prolong the privileged status one enjoys as a child, as the centre of attention. There were others prettier than me – not that I was stupid enough to think otherwise, but a woman, especially a very young woman, has a thousand and one ways of dismissing this obvious fact, through recourse to the conjuring tricks of seduction – but still, whenever I had to acknowledge the limitations of my body in a certain area, for example, the first time it was made clear that I was being passed over for someone prettier, I truly bit the dust. I actually bit the sheets on the bed where I buried myself, sobbing, and on occasions Claude's response was to kick me out of bed.

Neither of us was by nature talkative. Our inability to control our instincts, or to understand our emotions, was largely due to inexperience. The liberation of our bodies and our desires was an essentially expansive process, which would brook no obstacle; the slightest setback plunged us into a state of utter astonishment. However, another force sustained our dogged determination.

It was not a very great leap from the lower-middle-class world of the western suburbs of Paris to the art world of the Saint-Germain-des-Prés *quartier*, and the transition did not take long. There were no long years of study, no exams, no specialized knowledge was required, no collateral of any kind, just a predisposition, in Claude's case for business matters, and in mine for intellectual activity, and a significant share of per-sistance in both of us. To begin with we didn't earn much money, but this didn't stop us either from doing what we wanted to do, or meeting the people we wanted to do it with, so long as they were well-known characters. After a few years we left the studio apartment in the rue Bonaparte and moved to a large, bourgeois apartment in the Beaubourg *quartier*. Then there was the apartment in Milan. We weren't rich, but I was quite content if I could look up and see a nice high ceiling above my head, or hear my footsteps echoing on the marble floor in the entrance to the building. I did not need any more reality, just to be able to appropriate the signs I had seen in magazines or at the cinema. The little girl who dreamed over her books or at her window, or who never missed an episode of the TV adaptation of *Lost Illusions*, could believe, now she had become a young woman, that she had simply been waiting her turn in the wings and had passed through the stage door she had dreamed of, as if it had been no thicker than plywood. Childhood and adolescence form one long period of semi-sleep, during which the things we think about do not yet exercise any influence on our lives, because our family and educational environments offer no scope; our actions only become real once we have left this embryonic sac; in my case, all I had to do was wipe the dust from my eyes. So that the life we led, free of constraints, in a social milieu which at that time was one of the most welcoming and least conformist imaginable, was not an achievement secured after a long struggle, but simply by the expression of our desires. This feeling was reinforced, for me, by the fact that I easily came to terms with what had been, up until adolescence, my religious beliefs.

I had always adored those missals with gilded front edges, whose pages clung together like strands of hair when you tried to leaf through them, and padded leather covers, in which you could leave a neat little dent with your thumb. The one I had been given for my confirmation wouldn't shut properly, I had interleaved so many illuminated images, acquired at various baptisms and first communions, the kind in which Jesus addressed the onlooker directly, saying '*tu*'. These had played their part in the development of my taste for books, in the same way as the catechism had been a source of wonderful stories, from which I had gathered that if you had a deep and solid faith – the only difficulty being that of measuring the degree of your sincerity – your hopes would be fulfilled without fail, as though by the wave of a magic wand... My belief in

God had been so strong, I was convinced he had a special mission for me. I had the vague idea, for example, of a vast conciliatory undertaking. As my parents often argued, my task was to guide them back to a state of loving, and, furthermore, so to devote myself to others that I would lead them back to the paths of kindness and understanding; from this basis, I pictured my future in an environment in which peace reigned supreme. But this saintly vocation was no doubt just one more way of preparing for the life of a heroine, like those illustrated in my secular reading.

Then the presence of God vanished from my life. It is likely that my certainty that I had been chosen by him had prepared the way for the fantasy I mentioned earlier, of being noticed by a stranger, one who would single out, among thousands, the individual, male or female, whose potential talent would allow them to escape from ordinary existence. As it turned out, when I eventually found my way as a woman, and as a working woman, not by the intervention of the Holy Spirit but at least without reality trampling my dreams, when I saw the – to me – enormous divide between the future I would have had if I'd become a teacher of history and geography, or of literature, as my mother, for whom this would already have represented an improvement on her own situation, had wished, and this milieu in which I was not only in contact with artists, but where the avant-garde freedom in life and thought seemed to open up limitless possibilities, there seemed no reason to abandon my belief in my destiny.

Even when a human being has no belief – or has lost her belief – in the need to submit to God's law, if she sees her life conforming to a destiny prescribed on the opening pages of her imagination, she is no more inclined to question the path on which she is embarked than she would have been to question divine will. Whatever hardship and suffering I experienced during those years, it never led me to consider changing my life. I weathered arguments with Claude – rather like the anxiety linked to the copy deadlines for the printer of *Art Press*, the journal we had founded together – with the staying power of the long-distance runner, who is entirely focused on the necessity of maintaining his rhythm and reaching his goal. Being with Claude I had begun to realize the dreams I had nurtured ever since I had been capable of thought and I saw no reason to leave him, as long as these dreams continued to play out in my life, and as long as I could carry on dreaming.

waking dreams

From the beginning of my relationship with Claude I began the process of interleaving different layers of my life. I applied to my active adult life the same method I had used during the long wait of childhood, a method which had never failed me, a habit of interspersing my days with constant day-dreams of the most elaborate kind. These have become so essential to my equilibrium that I am sure that, for example, my inability to learn to drive is linked to an instinctive desire to make fullest use of those perfect opportunities provided by travel on public transport. Passive, captive, the body is set aside, just as it is during sleep, while we reserve, for the ever-changing representation of ourselves which we put in its place, a position which is often better, more controlled than in our nocturnal dreams. Who, moreover, on waking from a bad dream, has never tried to correct the unpleasant impression it leaves by allowing the unconscious or semi-conscious mind to supply its own happy ending? Anyone who, like me, has been so inclined, will know how much can be made of an open window on the overground train, offering a bold, fleeting glimpse of intimacy, or of those paradoxically secretive façades that slip by as the train passes through a provincial town, of those conversations between strangers on a train, upon which one intrudes while pretending to sleep. However brief the vision, however fragmentary the perception of our fellow travellers, a minute shred of ourselves becomes caught on it, and, just like those indiscreet television cameras which we pretend to believe are operated by an invisible hand, continues to force its way into the interior of a Parisian apartment, a provincial home, the domestic complications under discussion on the opposite seat. The dreamer refracts his own life. The world lays so many alluring or dangerously intriguing images before him, he wishes he could reflect each one of them, enrich it, fill it out, and thereby set it in perspective. The brief exposure, like the glimpse of a stage set, of the apartment or the provincial home, allows him to inhabit each for a few seconds, even if his own taste is utterly different; 'I am sharing the life of that family', he likes to imagine, with a slight shudder, if the discussion they are having reveals values he himself has always reviled. To some degree, the parents of a dreamy child are right to worry that the child will lack character later on, in the generally understood sense of 'rounded character', since the dreamer prefers to be several people, live several lives, many of which have no more substance than a speck of dust blown into the doorway of a house by a breath of wind. On the other hand, it is wrong to think of the dreamer as someone who turns away from the world, for very often his various lives actually give him a greater degree of empathy with it.

Certain daydreams, self-evidently, are erotic, and I was deep into this territory long before I became familiar with any actual sex acts, loosely associating them still with mouth-to-mouth kissing and hands on breasts. It is likely, too, that my natural disposition to daydream went hand in hand with a taste for masturbation. Ever since I was very young I have tended to fantasize elaborately and at length while masturbating. My fantasies are repetitive and become increasingly complex and labyrinthine with time, sometimes over a period of years, like those soap operas which run and run, with the writers making the plot up as they go along. I couldn't bring myself to orgasm without them. Having said that, not all my erotic daydreams are accompanied by an act of masturbation. The protagonists of the pornographic films in my head have features, physical and moral, which are both stereotypical and composite, and are drawn from a fairly broad range. Within certain categories – the owner of a bar or sex club, the businessman in a hurry, the group of idle young people, the foreigner who utters profanities in a language I do not understand, etc – I will cast from all ages and from a wide variety of physical types. Only very rarely are they manifestations of real men, people I know or happen to have met, or even film stars I swooned over as a teenager. Although there may be similarities between circumstances and activities I have known and those concocted by my imagination – and on some occasions the latter will strangely foreshadow the former, on others be inspired by them – neither my real-life partners nor my friends nor even simple acquaintances ever make their way into my daydreams. One of my masturbatory fantasies is incestuous. In this case, understandably, I think, the taboo is sufficiently strong for me to have substituted for the memory of my father's features, a body which is quite unlike his, and which is different each time. But broadly speaking, the taboo extends to forbidding me to summon up a stranger I might have noticed in the street. Obviously my characters must be composed of features belonging to real people, gleaned here and there, but such references are negligible or unconscious. Identification with one particular person is never possible. Even when I have happened to feel, and admit to myself, a strong desire for a man which has turned out to be impractical, or indeed impossible, to satisfy, I have never assuaged my frustration by recourse to fantasy. It is a curious fact: the realm of my daydreams is so tightly sealed, so radically out of bounds to any person whose identity is in any sense real to me, that even though I might gladly admit such a person into the intimate sphere of my real sexual activity, they would continue to be excluded from my erotic daydreams. I might invent a story in which I socialize with a man; I have a rendezvous with him, I imagine our conversation, but there my fabulation stops, before I get as far as suggestive words or gestures. I am incapable of using this means of removing the obstacle or taboo presented by real life, of deriving pleasure from this kind of mental transgression. If they are to develop freely, my sexual musings must have cast completely adrift, and I expect that the dreadful captain to whom, at that moment, I hand over the helm, would not welcome the sight of one among the crew whose face, summoned by a minute twitch of conscience, recalled the laws of *terra firma*.

Many of my amorous or sexual encounters follow a similar pattern to this one of flicking back and forth between real life and dreams. Perhaps it is precisely because seams of dream life are embedded between the layers of real life, pressing down upon them, but never merging, that life itself ends up being constructed like lamellar tissue. I was fortunate in that right from the start my life was held in place by a solid axis, supplied on the one hand by my work, principally the work for *Art Press*, the aims of which always remained clear to me, and reinforced, on the other, by my relationship with Claude, which, because we had in some sense embarked together on a social adventure, and also because it did not restrict our sexual freedom, had never been called into question. So, for some years, in parallel with this axis, I had pursued segments of various other lives, some of which had developed into long and deep relationships. I have written 'lives' and not 'affairs', because each of these relationships had a particular character-istic rhythm, set of rules and specific rituals. Each one allowed me to transport myself onto a different stage, to exploit differ-ent registers, like an actress: I might be bohemian, tart or *bour-geoise*, depending on the social position of the man I was seeing, and the social position he assigned to me, the friends he introduced me to, the restaurants he took me to, the activ-ities or work we met to pursue. Free from many of life's con-tingencies – as are most affairs to which the partners commit only a portion of their time, and as are adulterers, provided they are casual – these parallel lives held, for me, a charm similar to that of my daydreams; they were hybrid in nature; they gave substance to my mental images, but had none of the harshness of actual everyday life. In this way I visited coun-tries, frequented milieus, met personalities, not to say slept in houses, wore dresses, enjoyed perks which I might have vaguely glimpsed during the course of my daydreams, and I little cared that none of these privileges were actually features of a permanent way of life or lifestyle. In any case, I have always been fairly indifferent to status symbols, and the fact that I had tasted the vegetables at the Moulin de Mougins did not stop me tucking into a couscous in the bistro on the corner; similarly, though I had joined in orgies in the 7th arrondissement of Paris, I could still feel at home at a wedding reception in a small village hidden away in Umbria. The dreamer only hoards immaterial possessions, and attaches only limited importance to the fact that the object of his dreaming may by chance actually materialize, only to return once more to its immaterial state, in the form of a memory. In any case, he remains confident that the process can be reversed. I became very closely involved with Jacques during a period of over six years, while I was actually living with Claude, then I left Claude to live, initially, with a female friend who took me in, then alone for about three years, and then at last with Jacques, with whom I still live today. And it was not until the recurrent arguments between myself and Claude touched on the subject of the direction *Art Press* should take that I decided, one day, to remove my clothes from the large closet in our bedroom for good. When we decide, all of a sudden, to strike out on an unknown path, our determination is sustained, I suspect, by a kind of anaesthesia, since although I can see my clothes spread out across the bed, as though I were preparing to set out on a journey, I cannot recall what I felt at that moment. Perhaps it was my precociously early acquaintance with the great novels of the nineteenth century, a timely corrective both to the books which lull little girls into the expectation of a prince charming, and to the serialized love stories in the magazines my mother bought, novels which transported me into a society which in actual fact made no more connection between love and marriage than did certain ancient societies or certain long-ago peoples described by ethnologists, which we falsely pretend to be shocked by, as though their values were quite unlike our own. Or perhaps it is my nature, which is simple, one might say, primitive. At any rate, the fact remains that these basic requirements of mankind – the need to avoid solitude, to enjoy carnal pleasures, free of guilt or blame, but equally, to go beyond one's own pleasure into the realm of love for another person did not seem to me to be automatically or necessarily connected. I did not expect to satisfy them all with a single partner, I did not attempt to, or even imagine I might. Since, in that libertarian era, there were no secrets, it would sometimes happen – though rarely, it must be said – that people close to me would question my arrangements, or rather would express surprise that all my partners accepted them, in particular Claude, with whom I was living, and Jacques, who was himself single. I did not know how to answer them, since it was not a question I would ever have asked myself. However, although my secondary lives were not secret, they were, to some extent, separate. I would pass through virtual partitions, which I myself had set up, like Fantomas passing through the walls of people's houses, or a science fiction hero passing through the walls of time: and although I might take with me certain elements from one world, and tell tales of them in another, the people I dealt with were not supposed to have any personal acquaintance with the other worlds I came from and still less were they expected to remind me of them if I did not wish it. It was inconceivable to me. The truth, of course, is that it was I who deliberately, naively, turned a blind eye. Which is why these secondary lives were in one sense also dream lives.

I also chose not to look over the garden wall to where my friend–lovers were busy in other compartments of their love lives. I have already described how jealousy would suddenly flare up between myself and Claude. But nowhere else. I knew quite well that my male friends saw other women, had other relationships, and in some cases, wives. I knew some of these women as friends, or I might equally, while swinging, have come into contact with them sexually. I never had a particular emotional attachment to any of them. Of all the relationships I have had during the course of my life, they are the only ones from which emotions have been entirely absent, recalling rather that sense of moral well-being I have on occasions when I find myself having a conversation on a subject to which I am indifferent. I suppose I had neutralized their existence in advance. Not that they had no identity, but for me the mention of them evoked only bit players who did no more than cross the back of the stage and exit. For I set the limits of the stage and placed the actors in their positions, entirely according to my own convenience, and it little mattered if I knew my friend was married or was closely involved with another mistress, I was able, by a trick of distortion, to place my own mental image of my relationship with him at centre stage. Since for me none of these relationships was all-important, and I certainly never felt as though my entire life depended on any of them, none of my partners' affairs, either, could be considered a major obstacle, sending me back to my place in the wings. If I had had to explain myself at that time, I might well have happily claimed that the privileged position I routinely assumed to be my own derived in some sense from my ubiquity. I would have argued that I actually received more attention because people knew I might well soon drift off somewhere else, or perhaps, in my head, had already done so. I have learned since then that there is a form of egocentricity which paradoxically seeks not to focus on and strengthen the ego, but rather to scatter it and break it down.

The men I was involved with were no more secretive than I was, really, when it came to sex. Jacques was the one exception to this. His allusions to other women were rare and discreet and it was understood that I was not interested in asking questions. I was provoked to a variety of different reactions by the contrast between this mysterious part of my life and my own entourage, where the tendency was towards openness, a contrast which was the more noticeable because of the unique character of what I had begun to feel for Jacques. In the early days of our relationship there had been three or four occasions on which I had displayed jealousy. It was not at all the same kind of jealousy as that which had fuelled my crises with Claude. Although it is all a long time ago now, and memory has done a remarkable job of sifting and sorting, I am quite sure that until then I had never worried about a rival who might be more beautiful, or better in bed, than myself. The presence of an intruder shocked me: if the fact of her existence had emerged gradually in the course of conversation, or if I had just happened to run into her one evening, I would have had no difficulty reducing her to a generalized outline, but I felt crowded by her abrupt arrival on the scene. It felt like that absurd situation, only a thousand times more so, when you respond to a smile or a kiss from a friend some distance away, only to realize that the gesture was intended for the person behind you. Thus you discover simultaneously that you are not the only one who has a special friendship with them, and that sometimes they may simply not see you and you have to stand aside.

Early one morning I am alone in Jacques' studio after he has gone to work. Sitting at his table, in the bright light of the bay window, which illuminates the table and utterly exposes me, I write him a letter in a state of erotic fury. I have quite forgotten,

now, how I have just come to realise that Jacques receives fre-
quent visits from another woman in this studio. But I still
remember the image I employed to re-appropriate the space
and set my own imperious stamp upon it. Some time before
this, Jacques had burned his hands in an accident, and for
several weeks his movements had been impeded by two
stumps of bandage. So we had developed a habit of having sex
with him on his back and me sitting on top of him. I liked this
position, particularly when I could feel the slightly rough
texture of the bandages resting on my hips. In the letter, in
which I compared myself to the Eiffel Tower, straddling his
body, I asserted my exclusive right to this position. One's self-
awareness may so deceive one that, while being fully aware of
certain character traits or ways of behaving which we know we
tend to overplay, we fail to acknowledge the feelings they are
intended to repress. I am fairly sure that from very early on I
was sufficiently clear-sighted to know that the reason why I
placed sexual accomplishment at such a premium was because
I used it in the same way as someone who becomes hooked on
painkillers, not just to mask pain, but to get high. Despite this,
I could not have said exactly where the pain lay. It is the automatic reaction of the seasoned drama queen, this highly pol-
ished dividing of the self: I work myself up into a fever with
my copulatory locutions, while simultaneously watching
myself play out the role of icon of sexual liberation. I even
philosophise; in the almost non-stop dialogue I conduct with
the phantom tribunal which is constantly summoning me
before it, I explain that other values in life are insignificant, as
long as in this area one is prepared to pursue one's fantasies to
the limit. Having a self-image necessarily implies a certain
distance. Now, at this moment, that distance was not the

distance of a critical self-consciousness which, stepping backwards for a moment, addresses an aspect of itself, either judging it or, at least, subjecting it to irony; it was, on the contrary, a projective awareness, separating off from itself a sort of mannequin of its own making. I wonder if you will understand what I mean when I say that although I was present at the making of this mannequin (which is the opposite of its being un-made, even if it also demonstrates its artificial nature) this artifact was never-theless something to which I was inescapably drawn. The visible part of my consciousness needed to identify with a conquering figure, a Joan of Arc marching towards the spire of Reims, or rising up, why not, like the Eiffel Tower, because the other part, the part which I was precisely incapable of looking at, and for which, *a fiortiori*, it would take me a long time to find words (because the inner eye, like the organic eye, actually sees long before it can describe what it sees) kept bumping into the furniture of the minuscule apartment where this letter was being written, and from where this entire mental construct was being raised. Suddenly I had to make room for three in it, and actually for more: I had to let in the unknown face of the man who until then had seemed like the sincerest of all men, Jacques. In replying to my letter, he did not resort to metaphor. He asked me if I had ever wondered how he had managed the thousands of little tasks and movements of daily life all this time, without the use of his hands, given that I never spent longer than a few hours with him.

In the weeks after my break-up with Claude, when I was lodging with my female friend, in a cosy apartment under the eaves which would have made a good setting for two emancipated Truffaut heroines, I received messages of a rather more pressing nature from Jacques. They arrived at a rate of one or two a day, either by post or delivered by hand into my letter box. I always open my post, even today when, for professional reasons, there is an awful lot of it, in the same spirit of naked anticipation as that in which I receive surprise presents, even of the most modest kind, because, in a rather facile way, I invest the object of communication with the possibility of being such a huge number of different things that this potentiality wipes out any guess I might make based on what I might expect, or want. Alas, whereas a present retains its magic potential, providing I don't immediately dismiss the idea of using the useless gadget, or the hope that I might respond to the invitation even though I know my diary is already full, so that both present and invitation may act as potential interruptions in the organisation of my life, on reading Jacques' letters, which were at one and the same time urgent and – since written – delayed responses to a telephone call or to our conversation over dinner the night before, my mind immediately misted over.

I read them straight through, without stopping. I did not reread them, or scarcely. Having said that, I have kept them all. I read them in a state of panic. My eyes zigzagged down the page, I thrashed around among words which seemed to have become opaque. I might have reacted the same way if I had been attacked in the dark, flailing about, trying to seize hold of a hand, a sleeve, a flap of clothing, but failing, in the end, to catch hold of anything. During this period it was my firm belief that I would from now on be able to enjoy an even greater degree of flexibility in the exercising of my sexual nomadism, and I was quite sure that this also meant I would have more time to spend with Jacques. To him it looked as though I was turning into a kind of air traffic controller preparing to set up a vast network and he made it clear he was not interested in being connected. One thing which annoyed him, for example, was an idea I had for sharing a large loft space with one of my boyfriends: this man was an artist, and he could have had his studio in one part, and Jacques and I would have lived in the other. Jacques called it perversion: the naïve speculations of a woman who until now had thankfully managed to keep real life and fantasy separate.

I made no connection between love and sexual pleasure; nor, in my view, was pleasure single and indivisible. As I had always had several relationships on the go at once, I had never been concerned to measure the intensity of pleasure I derived from the sexual act with each one of my lovers, and if a practice I was fond of did not appeal to one of them, I would never have dreamed of insisting he go along with it. I knew quite well that a particular form of pleasure encountered with one man was not necessarily available with the next, but that the latter might, on the other hand, introduce me to a different pleasure again. Now, there is no doubt that what appears at first glimpse to offer a wider and richer range of experiences, in fact served to hold back the development of my libidinal personality. From this point of view, I was relatively slow in coming to know myself. What I have called the interleaving of the layers of my life entailed, as its corollary, the faceting of my libido. For a long time, through niceness, desire to please, curiosity, and various other reasons which were not solely connected to the pursuit of pleasure, I focused a lot on responding to the desires of my partners, while rather haphazardly satisfying my own. Passing from one body to the next, from one erotic world to another, my sexual persona adapted in a variety of ways, and I carefully managed my reactions. If I found myself able to respond to my partner's taste for a specific position, practice or role-play I would focus on working up that response, but I might equally well forget about it with someone else. I think this must be a faculty I share with many women who compensate for their traditional absence of initiative with a considerable, almost experimental degree of physical availability. The difference between myself and others is that I have changed partners more often. And while being very steady within my relationships, my friendships, my work, my intellectual pursuits, I was, unlike certain erotomaniacs whose rituals for achieving pleasure leave as little room for improvisation as the rules of monastic life, sexually versatile.

I could not put an exact date on the moment when, to put it concisely, my body separated out from my being. It became most clear that this was what had happened with the writing and publication of *The Sexual Life of Catherine M*. The success of the book accentuated the phenomenon still further. All writing entails a process of objectification, and in this case the aim had been to detail the maximum possible number of erotic situations and sensations experienced by my body. The book provoked countless reactions. Through this process of description and interpretation, the body of Catherine M. definitely ceased to belong specifically to me. But before even starting on the book, in order even to conceive of such a project, and before that, to commit to memory the scenes I recount in it, my inner gaze needed to be able to function in some sense as an outer gaze. In general, this so-called outer gaze is mediated; it passes through the gaze of another, who may or may not be present. The psychological circuit is extremely short, generally unconscious, but if I am in the process of 'looking at' myself, there, lying naked in this room, am I not imagining what someone looking at me sees, or would see if he were lying next to me? In this case, are not the mental images I have of my body and the position it is in, which I am perhaps trying to make conform to that mental image, already, to a large extent, reflections of the imaginative faculty of someone else? When we criticize someone for being narcissistic, we are usually ridiculing them for thinking they are blessed from the outset with such a beautiful body that their sole duty is to maintain it as it is, or at least to show it off well. This is a crude idea. The solitary narcissist who only has his own 'gaze' upon himself, and plunges into his own reflection exists only in the legend. The more common form of narcissism, to which, I think, my own belongs, is more modest and is quite prepared to submit to the principle of reality... I know, as do most of my brothers in egotism, that my attractions are unreliable, and that an appreciation of my appearance depends largely on the point of view from which you look at it. Now, points of view are provided by other people.

The fact that I consider my physical person as a sort of compromise between the ideal I inevitably forged during childhood and particularly during adolescence, the far vaguer puppet which succeeded it in my adult fantasies, and the patchwork made up of reflections in mirrors, other people's eyes and in photographic prints, has probably made me extremely flexible in my sexual relationships, while this same flexibility tended to accentuate the unevenness of my image. The conviction, which was never stated, but was nevertheless quite clear, that I possessed a floating body, distinct from my real self, the self we believe – probably in error, but we need to cling to the belief – represents our true being, and the versatility I showed during the early decades of my sex life, were mutually reinforcing. I shall try to be more precise by saying that I feel as though I have two bodies. One is the body I inhabit, or rather carry around, like a snail with its shell, without ever having really understood its relationship to the outer world (I don't drive, I can't swim; I am frightened of going downstairs in the dark, and I am forever twisting my ankle), whose needs and desires I must do my best to satisfy, whose aches and pains must be relived. Before going to sleep, I bury my head in my arm and am surprised by the smell, and when I touch certain parts of my body other than those involved in habitual gestures, such as the inner thighs, or the crease below the buttocks, they feel as though they belong to someone else. This body is a rather burdensome mass, which I can only really take the measure of once it has withdrawn: the impression left in a crumpled sheet, the empty place I leave behind and to which, on some pretext or other – reluctance to leave, fear I may have forgotten something – I return. I wonder, in fact, whether the moment when we recover awareness and the accompanying feeling of plenitude after the brief absence from oneself which is orgasm might not also belong to the same register. As for the ultimate withdrawal, the one which I will not be able to witness, I sometimes catch a glimpse of it, when, for instance, I happen to revisit a place where I lived for a long time, to which I have not returned for even longer. The immediacy with which the memory of my absent body imposes itself upon the space wipes out any other feeling, as though I had vanished into the ether and could at long last get a sense of my body in its entirety, from a point of view somewhere outside it. I am the involuntary, but accountable trustee of this cellular body.

The other body is the social body, the one which brings me into varying degrees of contact with others, and which promotes an image of me with which, in the end, each person is free to do what he will. The social body lightens the load of the cellular body. Whereas the latter carries weight and may create obligations for me, I am quite happy to delegate to others the job of shaping my social body, since it does not matter much to me whether I can recognize 'my self' in it or not. In front of the photographer's lens, I am an accommodating model, as docile as I was in the days when my mother subjected my recaltricant head to painful sessions at the hairdressers, or made me wear dresses she had thrown together on her sewing machine. Being of average height, average weight, with a changeable face, I have come across a diverse range of opinions as to my appearance, some flattering, others disparaging: too pointy for some, too chubby for others, while my face has been variously deemed affable, pert, or sullen. I can attest to a real pleasure in this kind of virtual mauling. Each time someone tears off a little shred, I am relieved of a fraction of responsibility for myself, for which I am thankful, since I am quite weighed down enough by the superego in the moral and social domains. Truth to tell, two pleasures combine here: I am fully aware that through the process of appropriation by others I am able to transcend my physical boundaries, and at the same time I can see that they are actually busying themselves with only the hide of me, while leaving me otherwise in peace, to pursue my inner dramas undisturbed. Mere tenant of the cellular body, liberal dispenser of the social body, I actually identify with neither one of them. This explains why I never felt that the coupling of this body with another body was equivalent to a commitment of myself. Whether the contact was a one-time thing, or regular, it was so easy to have at my disposal this fleshly emissary, whose function was to represent me in the world, and being confident that it was cool and detached, as indeed a good diplomat should be, I failed to see how any dire consequences could ensue. For this reason I was unable to understand Jacques' solemn arguments. He apologized for the inevitable use of the word 'passion' which, he said, should be understood in its 'quasi evangelical' sense, which had nothing whatsoever to do with the 'Feydeauesque' arrangements into which he accused me of trying to drag him. In an attempt to make sense of my comings and goings on the sexual circuit, and of my way of asserting my mastery in this field, his missives compared me to those ladies of the Middle Ages who made knights do battle in tournaments. He brought in psychoanalysis and in the end the words 'refusal of castration', 'hysteria', 'perversion' and long quotations from Lacan left me prostrate. On the one hand, I was prepared to believe Jacques knew more about these things than I did, on the other, these interpretations seemed disproportionate to what I had hitherto considered the simplest thing in the world – all the rest was so very complicated! I felt like an actress who has been asked to give up her career because she is suspected of having committed the crimes of Medea or Lucretia Borgia. Did I ever imagine that Jacques might stop seeing me? Did I fear that in order to keep him I would have to change my way of life? To be honest, I think I was incapable even of pursuing the argument that far, and that under the circumstances my divided nature did an amazing job.

I had always adapted readily to all sorts of sexual practices, and respected the personal moral code which each person, even the most inveterate libertine, follows in this department, without, of course, adopting it myself. With Jacques I accepted the rule whereby our relationship was exempt from the general system of sexual exchange – an exchange which was, perhaps, not so much physical as verbal, consisting in the naïve, not to say kinky, retelling of one's sexual adventures – within which I had operated until then, and in which, at the beginning of our acquaintance, at least, he had also participated. Once we had decided to live together, this acceptance necessarily had its impact on my way of life. I do not recall having taken any definite decision about it. But certain parts of me quite simply declared themselves free and independent of the part that was making this commitment to Jacques, and neither part ever felt the need to justify itself to the other. The need never arose. Jacques himself never asked any questions, and I no longer spontaneously told him all about my affairs.

I rather think Catherine M. must have been born around this time. I mean by this that the person I was with Jacques began to observe – with some distance, but close attention – the person, or persons I became when I was on a sexual spree, with the result that after a number of years of note-taking it began to add up to the material for a book. When I try to express the frame of mind I was in then, the nearest comparison I can think of is with the kind of vivid but unreal perception we have when, as the phrase goes, we recover our senses after having been unconscious. At that moment, objects at eye level appear enlarged and bizarrely close, and the voice of the person speaking right next to us echoes strangely loud in our head, and it is by reference to these amplified signs that we manage to situate our own body: on the ground where we have fallen, or to wherever we have been carried. Until then I had always enjoyed my sexual freedom as though it had been an innate faculty, but now I began to register images of myself via situations and encounters which, for the first time, appeared to me with the otherness of the picturesque.

Thus our lives take shape, not according to the convention which pictures a narrow ribbon of a road, leading to an invisible horizon, but as a series of layers, as densely packed as the earth's crust, and, likewise, permeable. Although I did restrain my impulses somewhat, I continued to maintain certain relationships, some of which led me into the kind of chance encounter which had long been a feature of my sexual practice. But as I did not share these practices with Jacques (whereas I had with Claude), they began to seem to belong to a sedimentary layer which was so remote from my daily life, so completely sealed off from it, that I began to feel like a speliologist. This is typical of the kind of paradox our conscience will accept, to enable us to live with our own contradictions: whereas certain dreams so thoroughly invade our sense of reality that they become as firmly rooted as proven facts, our minds, conversely, make us experience certain moments of the immediate present as though they were so far removed from our daily life that we would be quite prepared to believe we had dreamed them, or that they already belonged to the past, which justifies our treating them with as little importance as if they really had been chimera or distant memories.

There was a period during which the course of my life became so enmeshed with so many segments of other lives lived through as though in a dream, and so many daydreams, that the result was rather like a fabric where the pattern has been pulled out of shape; the fictional landscape aroused as much emotion as the real facts. These were the years after the

death of my father and, a few months later, of my mother, the
latter having been particularly dramatic, as it was self-inflicted,
and violent. For no reason I could identify, I noticed shortly
after these painful events – the second more so than the first –
and for some time thereafter, that I tended to drift into erotic
reveries of a kind to which I was unaccustomed. Until that
time, I had used my fantasies as an aid to masturbation, and I
had only ever evoked imaginary partners. Now I began to daydream in snatches, constantly re-running the same short, fairly
anodyne scenes, usually dialogues or seductive glances, flirta-
tious exchanges, signs which in real life, though small and
apparently insignificant, occasionally gave me such acute
momentary pleasure as to provoke an actual spasm, but which
would not have been sufficient to support an act of onanism.
Was it because I was now selecting the model for my fantasy
partners from among people who really existed, whether they
were part of my social circle or I had simply come across them
at some point, that I began to show such unaccustomed
reserve?

Nor did I feel the need to convert these daydreams into
reality. I have never been a flirt. And because I had always led
my sex life without restraint, I had become a fatalist; if a relationship was meant to happen, the opportunity would arise
without my feeling I needed to influence things, and if not,
the current of desire would flow away somewhere else, wrapping itself around a different branch. In this way, for a number
of years, four or five real people had doubles, in my fantasy
life; as it turned out, only one of them came finally to play a
role in real life, but such was the nature of this relationship
that, for as long as it lasted, it continued to feature more
prominently in my imagination than in my active life. He was

a moody man, who, as a lover, maintained a fine balance between delicacy and brusqueness, and then, for no apparent reason, would cease all contact, closing the door, never calling me on the phone. Perhaps this mysterious capriciousness led me for the first time to try tricks for snaring him which were thought out well in advance. I would find it difficult, now, to say how much time I spent filling up these intervals with fantasies, but I think I would be alarmed by the tally of hours spent working on strategies to break down his resistance or going meticulously back over our meetings.

I would plan out my days in such a way as to clear periods of time in which to daydream, during a journey, or a long wait I knew I would have at a medical appointment or treatment, exactly as I might have arranged a real meeting. For years I must have devoted my first and last thoughts of the day to laying my plans, and pleasurably anticipating their results, for I would later realize that I had managed to furnish weeks, even months of physical absence of the subject himself with virtual incident. Now, so great is the power of desire, and the resources of the imagination which support it, that four or five months of waiting, fuelled in this manner, were as rich and emotionally varied as if the man in my thoughts had actually shared my life during this period. This explains why he whose wait is long does not grow weary. Unless he is mad, and mixes up dreams and reality, his obsession will lend substance to his dreams, so they become solid walkways between actual events, while, quite often, real events, which may be too brief, or the source of disappointment, can come to seem more like dreams. What place do two hours of furtive caresses take in our affections compared to the length of days spent imagining the pleasure to come? Is it not in fact precisely the dearth of real facts which makes it necessary, by way of compensation, to bolster up our dreams? In these circumstances, the passage of time, that is to say, the succession of events which constitutes real life, does not make us weary of waiting, burying the products of our imagination beneath its own sediment, no, it favours their proliferation, so that the waking dreamer is as unaware of the passage of time as the sleeper, shut away in his nocturnal dreams. And when, one day, he does wake from the dream, it is not because he suddenly becomes aware once more of time. Nor do events shake him awake. Like the little cat who has come to cling onto our lap, pawing us for minutes at a time, concentrated and insistent on his pleasure, then suddenly, though no movement or sound has disturbed him, sits up, stretches, and disappears in response to a call which we cannot hear, so our own desire abandons its object. There has been no sign to warn us of our approaching detachment. I noticed one day that I had not seen the man in question for quite a while, nor had he featured in my daydreams. Only then did the notion of time return. I said to myself, more or less: 'Six months without thinking of him! I would never have thought it possible!'

Imaginative people pass through many an ordeal in their fragile little bark before capsizing in a real storm. While others come up against obstacles, or work out the route which will get them safely past, they find, without making a detour, a passage through which they can slip into a dream, and by the time the dream is over the obstacle will probably be safely behind them. Spared the struggle, they cling to these dreams, refuse to relinquish their desires, and maintain a child's blind faith in their visions. From the moment I found myself in a couple with Jacques, I adopted a general way of behaving which was much calmer than the one I had had with Claude. My temperament was better matched to his, and it suited me better to share the way of life and interests of a writer than those of an art dealer. There was also the fact that sexual permissiveness had tacitly become a taboo subject between us; that way we avoided the risk of jealous outbursts of the kind I had periodically experienced with Claude. Other people noticed that I seemed to have settled down to a gentle cruising speed. It was mentioned, for example, on a walk I took with Claude – with whom relations had calmed – and a mutual female friend. We had reached the age at which life seems to have crystallised, which does not mean that it is less full of events and emotions, but, because we are eager to put to use the experience of our youth, we tend to trap them in reflection and analysis. We were in Cassel for the Documenta, and were going to visit the Gemäldegalerie, which was in the castle overlooking the town. We had decided to walk through the terraced gardens and were making our way up through them slowly, partly because of the heat and partly because we were talking. I think the reason why I have not forgotten this moment, which was pleasant but, after all, insignificant, since I have quite forgotten what profound subject we were discussing, may be because the female friend expressed her admiration for what she called my wisdom. It is possible that in the presence of Claude, and the absence of Jacques, who had not come on the trip, I was making an effort to appear serene. Nevertheless, perhaps what I needed, in this situation as in others, was for someone to offer me an image of myself with which I could identify. I was undoubtedly happier with Jacques than I had ever been before, but I needed a personal viewing point from which to contemplate my happiness. One has to be able to take a step back in order to achieve a vision of oneself, arrived at by oneself, which, dialectically, because one tries to pin it down and in certain cases to improve upon it, ends up becoming the model to which one conforms. I was unable to step back from myself.

After all, I lived my life in all sorts of contexts, with all sorts of people, and this, because it meant seeing things from a different angle, should have altered my understanding. Added to which, as I have tried to say, the fact that I did not share all aspects of my sex life with Jacques had made me a more acute observer in this field. Nevertheless, each of my ongoing sexual friendships generated its own hermetic world, and it would have felt incongruous to me to use one as a pretext for asking myself questions about another, particularly about my life with Jacques. I may have made up a few more stories than other people, but each time I was so well and truly caught in the trap that I never stopped to wonder what I was up to, or indeed what anyone else around me might be up to. Equally, it never occurred to me that other people might also be pursuing their own storylines elsewhere.

the hidden envelope

One of the earliest texts written by Salvador Dalí in support of his theory of Paranoiac–Critical activity, published in *Minotaure*, is entitled 'Non-Euclidean Psychology of a Photograph'. Alongside the text he reproduces the photograph in question: two proud female shopkeepers and a man, somewhat in shadow, pose in the doorway of their shop; despite the 'hypnotic' nature of the central subject, the thing which attracts Dalí's eye and to which he draws our attention, is a tiny spool, a spool without thread, lying inexplicably at the edge of the pavement. 'This supremely exhibitionist object, by reason of its "imperceptible existence", lends itself both by its character and its invisible nature to the sudden irruption peculiar to "paranoiac apparitions" and cries out for an interpretation.'

Although, alas, I am unable to put it to the service of so great an art as Dalí's, I too have a certain gift for observation, thanks to which I also observe things which escape the notice of others. It is, of course, the light thrown on this gift by the painter's writings, and not simply the way it is expressed in his paintings, which prompted me to work on him. I find it easy to get my bearings in a strange town, not by following a map but by spontaneously noting a detail on a building or in a shop window at the corner of a street. When I open a magazine, I automatically identify the paintings and other peripheral objects in the photographs of celebrities at home; without even having to make an effort to do so, I make out the titles of the books in the bookcase against which they have been photographed. In the metro, I cannot help but notice the drooping hem of the woman climbing the stairway ahead of me. A friend I often used to stay with was amused by my ability to tell him where to find any object he might be looking for in his own home; because although I am not particularly indiscreet, and might at most have helped put away the dishes, my eyes would have noted the object, which, for me, held no interest, and the mental image, anchored in its setting, would have spontaneously registered in my brain. Note that this visual acuity is independent of the will of the person concerned, who therefore is justified in protesting innocence, saying that the unimportant object, the insignificant detail simply 'leapt out' at them. Dalí is right to say of the spool that it is 'exhibitionist'. The observer had not deliberately turned his gaze upon it, it is the thing in question which 'struck' him, that is to say assaulted him.

I should immediately qualify this. The assault will only occur, of course, if the conditions are right. Which psychological traits are encouraged by visual hyper-attention? In my work on Dalí, I mentioned two in particular (a more detailed study, you can be sure, would have identified more, which would interlink with these). The first and most obvious is sexual curiosity. By homing in on what is least obvious, the eye discovers what is normally hidden. Now, in our society the genital organs, the surrounding area and their activities continue to be thought of as best hidden. Should one's eye unexpectedly fall on a small spoon which the owner of the house has left lying around somewhere other than the dining room, this represents an invasion of the person's privacy, because at this point we feel very close to the deep, secret thoughts which distracted them; similarly the drooping hem grants us access to an untidy cupboard, which the owner would not dare to show to just anyone. This can cause us some embarrassment. In such cases, the little spoon, the drooping hem, are metaphors for the sexual organs. This would be the logical conclusion, whether unconscious or sublimated, of anyone who gives free rein to their scopic impulse.

The second trait I would call 'indifference to the organizing of the world'. Dalí takes this opportunity to attack Euclidean geometry, which not only governs our way of presenting the world through pyramidal perspective, but has succeeded in imposing itself upon our way of seeing, and even of thinking. If we are to remain sensitive to what goes on at the margins, and in the hidden corners, we must steer away from hierarchical systems which attach more importance to what is happening in the centre or at the summit, whether these systems go by the name of social, mental or aesthetic order. For example, with the photograph discussed by Dalí, we must suspend all interest in anything it might be telling us about a particular group of retailers around the beginning of the twentieth century; we have to choose to attend to the 'waste scrap', as Dalí calls it, which has fallen into the gutter, rather than to these three strange human figures. We must also disregard the beauty of the contrasts between the areas of light and shade in the image. In order to achieve this completely open-minded way of seeing, this perfect 'flattening out of reality', one must be one of those people who can move through the world guided by a kind of curiosity free of any preconception. Such a person rejects outright the distinction between interesting and uninteresting, noble and ignoble, beautiful and ugly. In his eyes, the world preserves something of the unity it possessed before the fall. Deep down, he is amoral.

The space in which Jacques and I live in Paris is arranged around one large room which, as in country houses, is given over to several different activities. It is the first room visitors enter; you leave your bag there and remove your coat; we cook there, we eat there; the high back wall is entirely covered with books. In the middle is a very large oval table which, because the room is a crossroads, is permanently covered with mail, press folders, catalogues and books, magazines and open news-papers which have to be pushed aside or removed at meal times. In the middle of all this jumble I had been aware, for several days, of an envelope which I immediately recognized as being from a photographic lab. It had been placed there, along with other letters. Jacques takes a lot of photographs and is always slow to get them developed. Whenever he turns up with the contact sheets I always enjoy getting them out of the envelope and looking at the shots, trying to remember where, and in what circumstances, they were taken. I had been tempted several times to suggest to Jacques that we should open the envelope that was lying around, and each time had been distracted by something else.

Retrospectively, you might think that he was being both straightforward and trusting, because it was Jacques who asked me to fetch something from his desk. On his desk I found the envelope, which had been moved. There was also a notebook. I am almost certain that the envelope had been opened and placed on top of the photographs, which were partially hidden by it; on the other hand, I can't remember whether the notebook was open or closed, since I claimed to Jacques that it was open, but I know that from that instant on, whenever we spoke about it, I switched between truth and lies with such sustained improvisatory skill that sometimes my memory can't decide. The shots were of a young woman with a camera in her hands who had photographed herself in a mirror; she sat naked on the floor with her legs open, and her belly was that of a pregnant woman. In the last picture of the series, the child had appeared on her lap. I recognized her as a friend of Jacques, whom I had met occasionally. Whether the notebook had been opened or closed, my attention would probably not have been drawn to it if the photos had been of a different nature. On the most recent page Jacques had written about a journey he was going to make out of town, and was saying how much he regretted that Blandine – who was not the woman I had just seen in the photos, but another – could not come with him. 'She's so beautiful!' he exclaimed, before going on to express his desire for her.

Very occasionally I had thought I could detect a certain sexual complicity between Jacques and a woman, sometimes I could see it happening discreetly before my eyes, sometimes a small detail or a third person would put me onto it. But the worry or concern which I felt at such times had never made any lasting mark. Jacques' place in my life was so clearly defined, and our relationship had always run so smoothly, that there had been no room, no scope, for worry or concern. And when I looked at the nude in the mirror and read the words of thwarted desire I did not remember any of these previous reasons for concern. Unconsciously, I steered clear of saying to myself: 'Here is proof of what I suspected.' I held at bay a surge of suffering, of the kind you feel all the more keenly because you know its causes have existed for a long while without your realising. Its intensity increases in proportion to the length of the period of blindness. I think I can say that looking down at these pictures and the words on the page, I felt nothing: shock is the best defence the psyche can produce in the face of an event which may prove too painful to bear.

I had in my mind a schematic vision which had not so far been challenged by a crisis: my rather dissipated personality countered by Jacques' smoother and more balanced one. Perhaps it was a vision based on letters he sent me just before we began living together, in which he warned me against the effects of my libertarian approach to sex. But this origin was also buried and forgotten; I hadn't thought of those letters for many years, and I certainly could not at that moment have joined together the total personality I believed they revealed with the mismatch of the photographs and diary. At the time of the events I am beginning to write of, we had been living together for many years, in a state of such serenity that I had never had occasion to touch up the mental portrait of Jacques which I had created for myself. Nor had I ever found myself wondering how I might interpret his behaviour and his words otherwise.

I came back to him empty of all feeling, pregnant with suspense. And it would be true to say that over the next few days this suspense unleashed a cascade of initial tearful questions, and went on over a period of months and years to asphyxiate our relationship. And yet I could never bring myself to formulate it properly, because I would have preferred him to respond even before I opened my mouth, or looked up at him.

I mentioned the photos, but not the notebook. Jacques' explanation was that he had a paternal relationship with the young woman. She had wanted him to have this record of her pregnancy. He thought it was odd himself, as he had never been particularly interested in the ideology surrounding pregnant women, and this I could quite believe. It was I who offered an explanation, in all seriousness. Some time earlier, he had published a novel, the front cover of which showed a reproduction of *The Origin of the World* by Courbet, and she had probably been playing at *The Origin of the World* in front of her mirror. I smoothed the surface of the table where we sat with the flat of my hand, and wondered.

To change the mood, we went out for dinner at the Café de la Musique. I like this place, an unlikely pivot between the Avenue Jean-Jaurès, with its unexceptional buildings, which loom too large, too solemnly, at night, once the traffic has thinned out, and the mass of the Parc Villette, with its few scattered residences, the odd light showing, and snatches of music which carry on the air. I have liked it even more since that evening, when the grey, rather sham-chic décor witnessed the disintegration of the woman, dreamer or schemer, unthinking or naïve, who was the partner, and, all things considered, happily so, of Jacques Henric. Not that the restaurant now makes me think with nostalgia of the woman I was until that evening. Far from it. Surprising as it may seem, it is more that I derive a dubious kind of pleasure from reliving the occasion of her demise. With a certain sense of indulgence I recall the feeling of dislocation in my limbs, which no longer seemed prepared to comply with the orders from my brain when I had to walk over to the toilets and push open the heavy door, and the irreversible unravelling of my consciousness throughout our conversation. It was as though I were carefully stripping something off me, like removing a plaster which one dares not tug off in one brisk movement, but peels away progressively, allowing time for each centimetre of skin to feel the sharp but short pain, a process which ends up providing a sensation which is akin to pleasure. Whenever I go back there I get pleasure from the reactivation of the pain I felt all those years ago now, as well as from observing that it has now diminished to a pitch at which it can be endured with increasing ease.

I find it quite impossible to recall how the meal unfolded, or what we talked about. I expect I was already trying to piece together the puzzle of the life we shared, but the only thing I could think of was the wretched act which had just overturned it. Apart from what I have said about my own disintegration, the thing I remember most clearly is a gesture of Jacques', when he upset his glass of wine and splashed me, and his suggestion that we go to a fashion show the following day, a presentation of lingerie at which Blandine would be one of the models. I still hadn't told him I had read the last page of the notebook.

Jacques went off on his trip out of town and at that point I started to read all his notebooks. I had noticed them a thousand times when I'd been looking in his desk drawer for a pencil or a piece of paper. I knew what they were, but they had never previously aroused my curiosity. The most recent ones were made up of Filofax pages in black bindings, and the oldest of them, some of them going back to a time before we lived together, were all different, some selected, perhaps, for their thickness and solidity, others, which looked like school exercise books, for their charm. There was one oddly shaped one, very long, like an old accounts book. The script was always fine, slightly cramped, with no margins. For a short while Jacques had kept his diary on his computer. That made things easier for me: the nude in the mirror was referred to simply as L., all I had to do was use the search key to discover all the times when Jacques mentioned going to see the young woman in the studio where she was assistant to a painter, when she was working there alone. Generally speaking, the journal was written in an elliptical style, the passages which were fully written out were few, but even so, I managed to glean certain facts, such as that he enjoyed having sex with L. on a pile of old blankets thrown down on the studio floor. Obviously I didn't read it all from start to finish. I had perfected my own form of speed reading which enabled me to identify all the feminine pronouns.

In the same way, I had trained my eyes to pick out, from a whole bundle of letters in a pigeonhole in a bookcase, any envelope covered in female handwriting. I developed a technique of removing these letters in bundles, so as to be able to put them back more easily, with the least possible disturbance to their random order. I would delicately remove one part of a pile, then stop still. Concentrating hard, I would let my eyes do the work. Slowly, I would examine the handwriting on the corners of the letters which protruded from the pile. Only when I thought I could see some handwriting which looked promising, or which I had already identified, would I put down that section of the pile and withdraw the envelope, letter or postcard, making sure, first, to take visual note of by how many centimetres or in some cases millimetres, it extended beyond the width of the pile, as well as of the angle at which it lay, so as to be able to put it back exactly later. These were absurd precautions. Jacques always seemed to me too busy attending to other people and society in general, forever busy with the detail of everyday life, looking at the objects he handles but remaining detached from them, because in his head he is re-reading the page of the book he has just put down, or looking at the invisible person with whom he is deep in conversation, to pay any attention to how things are laid out, whereas I am a good observer, in both senses of the word – both as one who sees and one who adheres to a rule. I could have conducted my searches far less carefully and he would certainly never have noticed. Even if I had knocked things over, buried an important piece of paper, he would merely have reproached himself for being clumsy or careless. And so, even if my intention was to leave no trace, some further explanation is required for why I took the art of snooping to such lengths.

Firstly, my emotional state was such that I could only move extremely slowly. Sometimes one's heart rate increases to a point at which it seems as though the heart is banging against the wall of the chest and that what one hears is the sound of it doing so. Before I could make any movement, I had to wait for the crazed organ in its cage to calm down. Or, as often happens, I used my lungs as an airbag, to contain it, and I would breathe very deeply. While I was glancing through the pages of a notebook or a pile of letters, I was caught in the grip of emotion; after that, the flawless extraction of my catch monopolized my attention. While I was reading, even though there was never very much to read, and I read quickly, I was in any case focused enough to forget about the reaction of my internal organs. I was far too busy with the hermeneutics of the laconic notes I was deciphering! Discovering the name to match the initial, putting a face to it, piecing together a set of circumstances and a precise place, based on a given date. And above all, translating two or three words used by Jacques into a whole dialogue, with gestures and speech, between him and the figure I had created, with more or less accuracy. Thus, for the first few days after the envelope which had been lying around had divulged its contents, I became the blind architect of my destiny, like an author who jots down vague ideas before the plot he is to become involved with takes shape, or a small, perverted rodent, collecting poisoned food! I built up a directory of situations, with accessories and related characters, while providing my fantasies with a whole workshop of images whose extent and cruelty I could not foresee.

And most of the time, I did it at floor level. On all fours, holding my breath, peering in at the pile of letters lying at the bottom of the pigeonhole at the bottom of the bookcase; either sitting or half-lying on the ground in order to take my samples and examine them. The notebooks were in a drawer higher up, but I still preferred to go through them in this lowly position. I avoided sitting in Jacques' chair, or, as a rule, touching the furniture or objects, even though it was unlikely that a police officer would be called in to take fingerprints. In the narrow space in the room under the attic roof, I huddled up small. Even as I watched these women, like actresses in rehearsal, marking out their steps on stage, sharing out positions in Jacques' life, I was reducing my own level of movement. Was it their virtual existence that kept me confined to the margin, was it an animal reflex on my part, bolting at the touch of unfamiliar hands? I methodically erased all traces of my contact with these women, even if the contact existed only in my own mind, like holding in my hands the writing paper which they had held, or intruding on Jacques' gaze upon their bodies. I completed the process of erasure by concentrating on this inadmissible activity, that is to say, which in theory, for the rest of the world, and sometimes for our forgetful conscience, is not meant to have happened.

I did admit it, though, in part. Jacques called me, and it was obviously easier on the telephone to tell him that I had looked at his diary. I suppose he realized how devastated I was, because, instead of saying he was shocked or hurt by my indiscretion, he talked to me gently. The sound of this measured voice was my greatest support at that moment. But I must still have been in the thick of it, because when he promised that when he got back he would tell me all about the affairs he had had with five or six women, my distress increased. I had not counted that many.

sarajevo, cluj, timisoara

Before Jacques returned from his trip I had to go abroad myself for several days. I was giving some lectures first, in Sarajevo, then making a tour of Romania. As I left Paris I was still mentally re-reading the passages in Jacques' diary, re-interpreting them in the light of what he had said to me on the telephone, continually dissecting the same fragments of dialogue, in the hope of pre-empting his promised explanations, but getting nowhere, my thoughts suddenly stymied by a failure of imagination, like suddenly hitting a patch of amnesia. I was growing increasingly familiar with the kind of misery which comes from doubting the person who has become the focus of all our interest, and which feeds, as we all know, on the fabrications we invent to fill up apparent holes in our lives, but also, conversely, on the state of perpetual expectation into which we are plunged, and which paralyses all our ability to reason, whether wildly or well. We suffer from our imagination, and sometimes even more so from our lack of imagination. I would soon repeat the same experience, over and over: I would myself come up with an explanation for a mystery in Jacques' life, after which there would be a moment when, perhaps because he denied it and I preferred to give him the benefit of the doubt, or simply because it seemed my suppositions were too speculative and must be abandoned, I would suddenly find myself devoid of any explanation whatsoever, literally face to face with the absurd. It is at such moments, far more so than at the moment when I would belatedly decide my interpretation had been over the top, that I would feel I was 'losing my mind'.

For example, in his write-up of a trip he had made to Athens, he described a very young girl who had performed an act of fellatio on him which, in its clumsiness, he had found both touching and exciting. I thought I recognized in his description the daughter of a friend who lived there. When I said her name, he rejected it so spontaneously, and laughed so good-naturedly, that I yielded to my own desire to believe him, for it is undoubtedly true that when we embark on this kind of painful investigation, we can usually be persuaded, by cowardice or exhaustion, to abandon the so-called truth we have been so actively pursuing. At the same time, I was as demoralized as if he had admitted it. Because, having answered so positively, he could recall neither the identity of the young girl, nor the episode itself, and I found myself in the strange situation of having to describe to him, relying somewhat on my recent reading, a scene which was taking such precise shape in my mind that I could have added to his written account all the details of the decor of the hotel room in which it had supposedly taken place, and which for him, even though he had experienced it, was a total blank. I would have preferred it if while I was trying to piece together his past, Jacques had taken over from me now and then and I could have sat back and listened to him. Of course, then I would have suffered not just from reading but also from hearing from his own lips, in his voice, touched by his emotions, the details of where, how and with whom, but at least they would have been obstacles which, once named, lost their allure, whereas Jacques' defective memory or his prudishness would keep me dangling in a void for a long time to come. The void made my head spin. I suffer from vertigo and it is true to say that weaknesses in an argument, or lapses of memory, what are termed absences, terrify me as much as a real precipice at my feet. When dizziness strikes, we cling to the parapet; if we are thrown into a panic by someone's refusal to speak, or by the incomprehensibility of life, we put up screens onto which we can project stories which will fill these empty holes. But sometimes these screens stay blank. As I failed to jolt Jacques' memory, the demands on my imagination increased, even as its ability to satisfy them faltered.

When I set foot on the tarmac at Sarajevo, I entered into an image I had seen so often on the television during the previous few years that I instantly recognized the hangars behind the airplanes from which the crates from aid organizations were being unloaded and important visitors were disembarking. The misery and dawning obsession I had been shouldering for the last few days suddenly disintegrated, and the particles went and settled on something I had never seen before, the recent marks of war: to the right of the road leading to the city centre, the shell-torn building of the daily newspaper *Oslobodjenje*, its feet wrapped in rubble and weeds; to the left the residential blocks, of which only two or three floors were inhabited, with a neat line of curtained windows across the façade, while the rest, below and above, was still blackened, the panes all shattered.

Has there never been a psychologist with the imagination

to borrow the principle of communicating vessels from physics and apply it to the laws according to which sometimes our personal torment spreads its black waters over the world and prevents us from seeing clearly what is happening, while at others the suffocating emanations from the world seep into us and make us swallow our bile? My memory of this time in Sarajevo is both emotionally powerful and happy. In a city emerging from a nightmare, my own distress was momentarily set aside.

Rather like certain mythological sites, such as those one visits in Greece or Turkey, unchanged from antique times, the city, because it is surrounded by mountains, struck me as having the proportions of a theatre set. Because they are built on a human scale, such places allow us to connect immediately with their heroism and glory; we feel as though we are walking straight into a page of a history book, and we mix this sensation with the silt of our personal recollections. Long afterwards, back in Paris, I realised that the feeling I had had when I walked on the site of the assassination of Archduke Ferdinand might well have had its origin in the naïve empathy I had experienced when, as a child, I was taken for the first time to see a play, *Imperial Violets*, at the Magador Theatre. This had greatly confused me; I had had difficulty distinguishing between what was and what wasn't part of the play. First of all I had been disappointed because I had believed that the Harcourt photographs of the actors which were displayed in the lobby were going to come to life, and my mother had laughed at my misunderstanding. The production must have been designed to impress, because they had real horses crossing the stage, and I couldn't work out how they had managed to get such big animals into such a small space. I was terrified later when a firecracker exploded to represent the bomb being thrown at Napoleon III's carriage. It was not quite the same period, and a different weapon had been used, but the confined nature of the place and the style of architecture, the plot of the story – an attack on a prince as he passed in his car – had, without my realising, fitted into the contours the earlier event had left in my memory.

For the present, I listened to the people of the city, who, having been unable, for years, to pass beyond their physical barriers, had acquired, through their sufferings, an openness to others, and hearing them talk about their lives, which had been lived partially underground during the siege, gave me leave from the psychic imprisonment I had been in before my arrival. At certain moments I even had the pleasant feeling that I was starting to float upwards, because the room in which I gave my lectures was in the dome of a former church, now the headquarters of the Soros Centre. It was the end of winter, the weather was sunny, and light came in through windows all the way round the room, and it was only in the mornings that my worries came back, in my hotel room, when, in the blinding light of the single curtain, which was orange and transparent and was supposed to hide the window, I called Jacques. The light had woken me early and burned my eyes. The connection was good. Our conversations were friendly and lasted five or ten minutes. But Jacques gave me to understand that we couldn't spend this long on the phone every time.

As my journey continued, I began to feel like Jonah taking refuge in the belly of the whale. After Sarajevo, in ruins, but still hospitable, in its basin, I went on to Vienna, from where I was to take a plane to Bucharest. At that time I often went to Vienna, the centre of which, circumscribed by the Ring, has

also preserved its human proportions. There I felt truly in the
belly of Europe, the more so because the airport is a crossroads
for Central Europe and the Balkans, and the departure lounge
(for Zagreb, Budapest, Bucharest, Sofia, Warsaw or Minsk…)
where I often found myself, is itself shaped like a rotunda. In
Vienna I spent a night at the house of some friends who gave
me a little room which could have been that of a child. With
the sheet and the cover over my head, speaking quietly, I had
a much longer phone conversation with Jacques. I asked him
to caress me, he replied that he was going down on me, I must
raise my legs high so he could get a proper hold of me, he was
licking my pussy. Was he rubbing himself? Yes, even a little
'suck' from Catherine would be welcome. I was touching
myself too, I slid in my middle finger, it was wet in there…

However, during masturbation, I can only reach orgasm by
using fantasies, and I have to work them up with such precision that it is almost impossible for me to reach orgasm in the
presence of a witness, even if they are only listening, because
the slightest word from him, the sound of his breathing, even,
will disrupt my concentration. Sometimes, when I sense the
emergence of contradictory feelings, the fear of wearying my
partner, because I am decidedly slow to bring my stimulating
tale to term, and a certain hostility towards him, because he is
stopping me from getting on with the job on my own, I prefer
to give up. So I am sure I did not climax during this exchange,
in which my hand was not simply responding to the images in
my head, but was also being partly loaned out to Jacques. I
came after I had put down the telephone. I don't remember
what images I used.

. . . . .

In Bucharest my hosts told me at the last minute that I would be travelling to Cluj on the night train, instead of by plane, as planned. You couldn't depend on the plane, and since my schedule was tight they didn't want to risk my being late. There was no time for further explanation, a driver took me to the station and put a ticket in my hand. I found my train, and my compartment, which I was sharing with a rather large blonde woman with a youngish, pleasant, pudgy face. She spoke French, even taught it, she told me, in a gentle voice. She held her head slightly on one side, like someone who is shyly making a request. She chose the top berth.

Suddenly the moment of grace afforded by my stay in Sarajevo and the stop-off in Vienna came to an end. I was irritated by the prospect of spending a night in an uncomfortable train. The journey was beginning to tire me. The carriage jolted about terribly, the heat in the compartment was stifling. I couldn't even get to sleep, and in the damp, dark net of the lower berth, dimly conscious of the creaking of the platform overhead, I began masturbating, continuing on throughout the hours of darkness. Scarcely had the aching muscles of my hand loosened up after having brought myself to orgasm than the imperious desire to start again seemed to stretch once more across my lower belly. My fingers were swimming in a mixture of sweat and vaginal moisture which, when I parted my sticky thighs, made a small dry sucking noise which made me fear, just as I did as a child when I aroused myself lying next to my mother in bed, that my fellow traveller might hear and guess what I was up to. I do not remember seeing the strip of daylight appear at the bottom of the thick curtain over the window; I must finally have succumbed to sleep.

I was an imaginative onanist, expert in the elaboration of a broad range of erotic reveries. But on that ancient train, during those chaotic hours of night I found myself being ingested by amoeba-like characters whose faces and names I knew, and who were taking over the theatre which until then I had occupied with solely anonymous accomplices. From that night onwards, I who had always been so inventive, found myself subject to even stricter rules than those imposed on classical authors, with fewer devices for getting round them than the latter allowed themselves. For a long time afterwards I could no longer achieve solitary arousal without recourse to the exasperating image of Jacques' member penetrating one of his girlfriends. Already I had ceased to feature at the heart of the action in these reveries, now I was merely a spectator. If I did participate, I would quickly find myself being excluded. I could now only trigger the deep internal wave at the precise moment at which my mental computer had Jacques arching backwards, making a grimace of pleasure as he climaxed.

How long did this routine last? Two years, three years, maybe longer. A long time, during which the world of my libido was turned over to invaders. Images of Jacques, now with his succubae clinging to him, replaced all scenarios featuring myself. The standard types who had featured in my masturbatory reveries until now were no longer sufficient to excite me, and the stories I had been developing for years, in numerous variations, some of them since childhood, were completely abandoned in favour of those dictated by the few brief passages lifted from Jacques' notebooks. In other words, the range was considerably reduced.

I drew principally on certain scenes set in our house in Paris, and in our house in the Midi. Where the text of the diaries and the letters were unspecific, I would transpose the scenes mentioned to one of these settings. Whereas in the past I had always dreamed up decors based on distant memories, on houses and gardens I had visited or seen in films, and lodged in my mind, or places which were perhaps more familiar to me, but public, and thus out-of-bounds settings for lewd acts, the space in which my reveries played out shrank to the few square metres of our homes. Until this point, the taboo which kept the people I regularly encountered in everyday life at a distance from my fantasies also extended to my domestic quarters; my fantasies stopped on the threshold. This taboo, likewise, went out the window. This limited the situations to five or six sites: the entrance hall of the house in Paris, the counter at the front of the kitchen area, the sofa in the living room and another in the house in the Midi, the two garages, the one in Paris and the one in the Midi. Later, I added the home of one of our very close friends outside of Paris when I learned that Jacques had gone there with one of his young women. Any scene set in one of the bedrooms would be richer and more developed than the others, on a par with the trauma the discovery of the episode had caused me.

Each setting had its corresponding and precise position: on the sofa in Paris, Jacques was taking the girl from behind in broad daylight, by the windows, in the other she was lying on her back, a pale patch against the verdigris fabric. The upper half of her body was between his thighs and he was pushing his sex between her breasts. The inspiration for this last image came not from reading his diaries but from two or three phrases that Jacques had let slip when I questioned him on the telephone, which had left a marked impression on me, the more so because this was a practice which my body made impossible, in other words, a form of pleasure which I had never imagined he might seek. In other fantasies, he took the girl standing up, just with her skirt raised, behind the counter, and similarly in the garage, where she stood with one foot resting on the running board of the 4 by 4. In the corridor, they fucked on the concrete floor, hastily. I always 'saw' these scenes of copulation from behind Jacques, that is to say, I saw his back and buttocks from a slight distance, I watched the movement of his pelvis, his hands gripping the fleshy part of her hips or her breasts. The girl's body was far less distinct, partly hidden, her outline never very clearly defined. The scene on the sofa in Paris was the only one into which I put myself, at least to start with. The set-up was classic: while she leaned forwards over the sofa, to give a better angle on her rear, I would come and place my sex within reach of her mouth. This intrusion on their coupling was a brief manifestation of the need for revenge, for I pictured myself directing operations, telling the other protagonists what to put where, but this fantasy did not last long. In reality, I have never been the one in charge of manoeuvres.

I was more at home in those scenes where I stayed hidden, a voyeur, an eavesdropper, in those where my exclusion was underlined, in a manner which bordered on cruelty. Examples: I would come home unexpectedly and on the stairs leading to the living room would hear the couple moaning and groaning; of course they were far too involved in what they were doing to notice my presence, and I stayed there watching them from behind the corner of the wall. I entered the room at the very moment Jacques had his orgasm. A subtle embellishment sometimes had him shooting off the very second they both noticed I was there, with a glance behind them, his final thrust breaking through, as it were, his astonishment at seeing me watching. However, the best hiding place was his office, on a mezzanine above the living room, or better still, the low-ceilinged attic, which you entered via his office. From there I listened to them, rather than watched them, harking back, in my fantasy, to the place and the position in which I'd carried out my illicit searches.

The telephone cut in on the scene where he was masturbating between her breasts. I pictured Jacques picking up the telephone to answer my call and, without breaking the rhythm of his thrusts, talking to me about the kind of trivial matters which enable established couples to maintain their intimacy during periods of brief separation. I was completely sidelined: I was not present, physically, Jacques' anodyne conversation hid the situation from me – he was making fun of me – and as I had never actually seen him take his pleasure in this way, I felt as though, rather like certain fairy tale beasts, he was suddenly revealing a side to himself which I had never known existed. Worse, or better, still, the duplicity which I attributed to him was a complete reversal of the moral qualities I had always seen in him.

I realize the vaudeville-cum-hardcore nature of these various scenarios now that I come to write them down. If I had been aware of it then, I do not think it would have put me off, since I know that my masturbation always went best when fuelled by situations which were extremely stereotypical and, if possible, downright degrading. The difference with vaudeville was that no scene of scandalous discovery arrived to put an end to their evasions and pretence. The reverie stalled on the image which was the signal for my own orgasm, that of Jacques' ejaculation, which, in its precision, showed everything, down to the last detail of his tautened muscles or the tensing of his face. If I ever did pursue it further, because I had not reached full satisfaction and was prepared to allow my mind to drift for a moment before resuming my story, or because, once my pleasure had subsided, my thoughts reverted to their regular morbid course, I imagined leaving the house without a word, leaving Jacques and his companion in a state of shock, and walking straight on for hours, until I reached the Paris city limits; I continued on into bare countryside and collapsed from exhaustion. A variation which did not fit together very well with the previous episode had me leaving naked under a coat or raincoat, even in bare feet, heedless of the cold and the rigours of the road. My nakedness was like a refuge, a protection. Voyeurs like to enjoy their pleasure alone and masturbators are voyeurs who prefer the comfort of their mental visions to the danger of satisfying their urges in real life. But it is true of both that they can only devote themselves to their activity by removing themselves momentarily from the public arena. And if they don't manage to be entirely secret, people condemn them, forcing them to be even more secretive still. Even if circumstances exist in which they are tolerated – in an orgy, for example – a kind of atavism requires that this exclusion and stigmatisation must eventually be a feature of what pleasure they find there. Surely in my vision of myself as a woman wandering alone and lost, implicitly driven from her own home, although my hand never strayed to my sex, I was achieving the acme of solitary pleasure?

A sleepless night on the train between Bucharest and Cluj was all it took to establish the elements of these mini-stories which would later be repeated a thousand times over. It is a shame that we cannot summon up memories as we might visit a museum, because faced with the models elaborated by our psyches from our earliest years we might feel the same sense of amazement inspired by primitive works of art, because they effortlessly present a formal perfection and an expressive quality quite equal to the art of later centuries, which for so long we wrongfully saw as the fruit of experience acquired by successive generations. What is true for humanity is also true for the individual. Maybe if we had better recall of our child-hood nightmares and the ghosts which featured in our early anxieties, we might find some consolation, or fitting compen-sation, perhaps even grounds for pride, in the fact that the dreams were so well crafted. Would obsessions which haunt us in our adult lives not be less painful if we were able to admire the perfection of these primitive constructions of which they are no more than an echo, and congratulate ourselves on our precocious, but nevertheless accomplished authorship? What narcissistic satisfaction would lie in repairing our psychic ills! I come back to Salvador Dalí: our paranoia need not be as great as his for us to follow his example, and rather than submit to the threats of others, we would do better to give some thought to our infant terrors and to emphasise the degree to which, in their very hyperbole, they can be wonder-fully coherent and explicit. During the next few years, as well as remaining unchanged, except in the details, the fantasies I have just outlined also grafted themselves onto patterns which went back much further. I was not deceived by this. Thus, one of my recurrent memories goes back to a time where I was scarcely pubescent. It was a Sunday with the family, that is to say, because my parents did not get along, and therefore never went out anywhere together, in the company, that day, of my father and brother, my aunt and my parental cousins. After a picnic in the park of Saint-Cloud we played boules. There were a lot of us, all excited by the game, and it happened that my turn was skipped, and no one noticed, except me, of course, but I said nothing. I have never forgotten the wounded feeling of being excluded from the game, airbrushed out by the others. I have never forgotten it because I have continually sought to revive it. That day, I ended up reminding them of my presence, but almost reluctantly, and the apologies and the comfort which were offered could not compete with the spasm which had clutched at my heart a few minutes earlier.

I had already experienced this state of compulsive onanism when suffering from cystitis (or bladder-burn). If you really try hard you can convert the irritation into arousal. But as soon as the arousal has expired, you have to start rubbing all over again, because the irritation then becomes even worse. Added to which, pleasure obtained in this way rarely reaches a point of saturation, and each time it ebbs it leaves an even bigger emptiness, which I experienced as a wound opening in my body and almost cleaving it in two. Was it this feeling which made me adopt one particular gesture? Not content with rubbing my clitoris, I also press it, and rub the two lips of the vulva together as though trying to suture a wound. In the case of cystitis, the desire to urinate fostered by the irritation becomes a sort of prolongation of the arousal, and one can even have the feeling that urination is finally going to help you realize your pleasure. In the train I must have gone to the toilet six or seven times. Fortunately, our compartment was at the end of the carriage and it was not far to go. If, for all the care I took in opening the door, my companion woke up, she must have thought I was unwell.

The train dropped me at Cluj, in that woolly mood left by bad dreams, which hung around for the entire two days of my visit. It must be said that my first glimpses of the town were unreal. In the car of the director of the French Cultural Centre, who had come to meet me at the station, I noticed that at certain times we were driving over beaten earth; we would pass carts whose drivers, small and hunched, wore astrakhan bonnets. I wondered how I came to be here, to give talks on the absolute 'cutting edge' of contemporary art. The director invited me home for breakfast, which I had with his children, whom he was trying to hurry to get off to school. At last he drove me to the apartment which had been placed at my disposal in a building far from the centre, one of these blocks which the communist countries managed to make even more basic than those in France. From my window I could hear the cocks crowing on nearby balconies. I decided not to take a bath because the water from the tap was rust coloured, however long you let it run.

The historic centre is very fine gothic, baroque, white. At the School of Art and Design, I spoke in a large room with exposed beams. It was packed out, and the audience listened without the need for an interpreter. I got on well with one of the women teachers. I had to go back to Timisoara by car, and she decided to come with me, as she was keen to continue our conversation. She would return the same way, since the driver had to bring the car back to Cluj anyway. Sitting in the front, my eyes roaming over landscapes which might have been drawn by illustrators of fairy tales – a narrow road winding between twin rows of trees, like the one which leads to Sleeping Beauty's castle, a chain of breast-like mountains which might have been the one over which Puss-in-Boots strides, I let myself go, running through a few new scenes from the story of Two-faced Jacques. At the same time I continued to talk with my companion, who was of a reserved and peaceful character, which allowed me to get on with elaborating scenes of a less sexual and more sentimental nature than those I had dwelt on in the train. These new fabrications did not reflect the written documentation I had had access to, they were pure invention, as anodyne, for example, as kisses, tender, mechanical gestures passing between Jacques and his friend whenever they met at an arranged place; inspired, in fact, by our own behaviour, his and mine, when we were together. Furthermore, I mingled these visions, in which a stranger took my place in the relationship of close-knit couple, with identical ones which looked forward to our affectionate reunion on my return. This embroidery went well with the spirit of resignation of my companion, who talked in measured tones about her research into contemporary stained glass, and the price of petrol, which had just doubled, which was why she couldn't use her car, or travel in order to complete her study. I promised to send her some literature to read. An excess of conscientiousness fuelled my words, as the voluptuous pain aroused by my fantasies spread through my body in that particular way, where we are unsure whether our internal organs are gently contracting or, on the contrary, dilating. It was hot inside the car. I abandoned myself to that perfect beatitude described in the *Lives of the Saints*, the reward of those who bow to the divine will.

At the time of this trip, the events of December 1989 were still very fresh in people's minds. To go to Timisoara was to visit the site of a revolt, of its repression, and of the macabre drama into which the revolt had spiralled; it was like going back to the source of the brownish water which ran in my basin in Cluj, living proof to the humanity of the late twentieth century that there would never be enough clear water to wash history clean, echoed in the very name of the town, a word which sounded like a lament. There I met a young female colleague, who I remembered with some emotion, because when I first met her, some time before at a colloquium in Budapest, the woman acting as moderator had so violently laid into her, right in the middle of her contribution, that she had burst into tears in public. Only two of us, a young German woman in the audience and myself, came to comfort her after the session, suspecting vaguely that the incident was a kind of remnant of the much longer history of relations between Hungary and Romania which had emerged without warning. She was my guide now in Timisoara for this last stage, blonde, calm, with a slender pre-Raphaelite form, a light in the darkness of the vast but comfortable Jugendstil apartment she lived in on Victoriei Square. I decided at last to take some photographs with the little camera I had brought with me. On my return I would be able not only to get swiftly back to the discussions I had begun with Jacques before I left; I could also show him my holiday snaps.

If I had been able to achieve a bit more detachment from my obsessions and proceed to some self-examination, I would have empathized with my friends in Sarajevo, and with my Romanian escorts, in connection with an encounter I had had two months previously, a long way away, in Buenos Aires (we art critics get around a bit). In the plane I had read from cover to cover the novel Jacques had just published. I am not always as acute as my eye is sharp – as you can see from this book – but, even so, I can be, with literature or works of art, including works by people I am close to. This is perhaps a faculty which goes with being a critic, a job which has wholly possessed me, to the point where it is second nature, but perhaps my choice of profession chimes with my habit, adopted in childhood, of living inside my head, in a world fuelled by observation. The result is that when I am faced with objects which invite evaluation, I do so as though I were a visitor, so to speak. Because my aspirations, my objectives, are focussed on my inner world, I can be relatively impartial with regard to the outer world; my disposition, perhaps, has made me into one who, the better to judge, must stand outside. I have always read Jacques' books as if we have nothing to do with each other and I would not have much difficulty in pointing to what in my opinion were the weaknesses or tics, as well as the qualities of his writing. This time I was full of admiration: it was the happiest of his novels, and at the same time, the most serious. The finest, it seemed to me. I also noticed, but did not make much of, the fact that the character of C., who had appeared in all his previous books, was missing from this one.

As soon as I arrived, I became caught up in the environment I had come to visit, and I struck up an acquaintance with a lady who was a curator of a museum in Athens, who, like me, had been invited to the conference. I don't know whether she was older than me, but she seemed so, with her maternal appearance, her two-piece suits and her smooth chignon. She told me her story: she had been recently widowed, she had loved him and he her, and he had died very shortly after they were married. Why was I so touched by the grief which filtered through her perfect reserve, that school-mistressy manner which is so unique to mature women? Why did her company seem to open up a valve in me, through which the life I lived together with Jacques escaped? She asked me about this life, and said she envied me, but during the course of our conversations, far from appreciating how fortunate I was and drawing comfort from it, I felt as though it was incredibly distant and almost unreal. My memory of this conference is dominated by this feeling. There was a reception on a terrace from which you could gaze across the whole of Rio de La Plata; I can still see it. Under different circumstances I would have adored this sense of taking possession of the width and breadth of the world, but while everyone was busy screwing up their eyes in an attempt to see Uruguay on the opposite shore, I kept my distance and merely observed that the view was not at all picturesque. On the final day, my friend of the moment gave me a present of the records of Tita Merello, Ada Falcon, Azucena Maizani, nothing but heartrending tangos.

By sharing in the unhappiness of others, we are sometimes able to protect ourselves against the unhappiness we vaguely sense is hanging over us; compassion can serve as a distraction. But when suffering already has us in its full grip, we may derive not so much consolation as a paradoxical euphoria from the discovery that we aren't alone. When I came into contact with people who were deeply unhappy, or had recently been through great adversity, my own misfortune became diluted, but not dispelled, so that it was rather like adding water to a cup of very strong coffee – apparently this heightens the stimulant effects. Submerging myself in the world's unhappiness did not make me less sensitive to the unhappiness I believed to be my own, it simply intensified it subconsciously. Perhaps I was fascinated by the kind of love mentioned by the woman I met in Buenos Aires, a stable and profound love, experienced in the full maturity of life. Perhaps, beyond my present anxiety, the seed for which had just been sown by the disappearance of C., I aspired to such a love.

Of course, the dramas experienced by my friends in former Yugoslavia and Romania, the difficulties they were faced with daily, helped me put my own pain in perspective, but both had expressed themselves in words which I myself could have used to describe my own feelings. As for the ostracism inflicted on the young Romanian woman in Budapest, which I remembered when I met her in Timisoara, its causes were quite remote from the events which made me imagine that Jacques was pushing me away. But the mixture of sadness and fighting spirit in her inclined me to identify with her, exactly in the way we delegate to the characters in plays or films, embroiled in plots which have nothing to do with us, the power to feel and act in ways we would not dare allow ourselves in real life. More generally speaking, we all constantly observe our fellow creatures, and interpret their actions in the manner of an author who develops the plot of her story, distributing her own feelings among the various characters, making them express her own concerns, or even resolve her conflicts.

There even exists a perverted form of this phagocytosis, by which, having seen another person express their feelings in a certain way, one decides to adopt it oneself, even though it is not the way one would normally behave, and one might even possibly find it vulgar and despicable. Long after these travels, I was in a taxi one day and found myself, to my surprise, starting a conversation with the taxi driver which was almost intimate, whereas normally I stick to small talk. He apologized for being a little distracted, saying that he had just split up with his girlfriend. I replied that I myself had recently discovered that my husband had cheated on me. The words 'husband' (which I scarcely ever use, save for administrative purposes), and 'cheated', used on this occasion myself for the first – and last – time, and also my replies to the man's questions and the sympathy he expressed, gave me the syrupy pleasure of slipping into utter cliché.

Pleasure is felt most intensely and pain most profoundly when they call into play a maximum number of emotional channels and tap an incalculable number of happy or unhappy memories, of dreams which have come true or been broken. So it is troubling to realize that these contradictory and complex emotions have exactly the same effect on the gut, not only that, but they actually work in the same way as the most basic of all reactions – fear in the face of physical danger. One might say that our intestines function according to primitive software, which is incapable of recognizing the new, sophisticated programs running in our brains, and which translates them into a jumble of rudimentary signs. Some people have surprising psychosomatic reactions, sudden hair loss, for example, or the development of bizarre allergies. But most of us usually experience only a visceral reaction – in a literal sense – which does not distinguish between fear, happiness and unhappiness. For a long time, I couldn't give a lecture without my digestive tract obliging me to pay a visit to the lavatory a few minutes before the start. Now, an incomparably worse drama, such as the loss of a loved one, could trigger exactly the same effect on my intestines in short order. Should one be ashamed of the way one's body disregards the hierarchy of emotions drawn up by one's rational self, and mangles them all up together? Would it not be better to take pride in the way the body ignores the moral, sentimental and even intellectual values which have gradually bested our emotions, and restores us to a state of reason, that is to say, to a recollection of our true nature, which, in the process of its decay, will drag down all these values with it? The discovery which had bowled me over in the days before I went abroad had thrown me into total mental chaos, which had had its impact on my gut. And this generalized chaos had made me lose my adult regularity and partially return to the state of indifferentiation which characterizes the early months of life. In short I must have gone to the toilet and forgotten to flush.

By chance, Jacques and I arrived home from our travels within a few minutes of each other and I found him opening his suitcase. This is how the scene unfolded: as I open the door I see him turn round, at the end of the dark corridor, in the light of the room. His eyes are full of tenderness and a slightly doubtful expression plays around his mouth. I say nothing; I come and sob on his shoulder, something which has never happened to me before; he kisses me and says several times 'my darling', a word he doesn't often use either. And then, after a short while, when I have finished crying, he asks me if I was ill before I left. No, I wasn't. Then he indicates the state in which he found the lavatory. He tells me gently, kindly, and is reassured when I look at him, astonished.

c. missing

The way to Jacques' study was up a metal spiral staircase. For months, this spiral exerted a force of attraction on me, against which I constantly had to struggle, and which, I'm afraid, almost always got the better of me. It was enough for me to be alone in the house and for my movements to bring me within sight of the staircase. As it is situated directly opposite the door to the bathroom, I necessarily passed very close to it, several times a day. Sometimes I forced myself to go past without looking, but just as I was about to enter the bathroom I would often turn about and start to climb. Once I had got past my moment of hesitation, I went up quickly, almost trying to get it over with. I was not on automatic pilot, more like a subaltern who is conscientiously carrying out the task he has been assigned. One version of myself had briefly struggled with her conscience and reached a decision, another put it into practice, without pausing to reconsider. And, as has been said before, Pandora was not intending to rummage, but to conduct a serious investigation.

It was not my conscience which made me pause. Of course, when I was outside the zone of attraction, I promised myself, each time with the same degree of conviction, that in future I would resist the impulse; my lack of discretion was hateful; if Jacques found out he would feel justifiably bruised by this violation of his privacy. But these were thoughts which came from a somewhat forced super-ego, a catechism I resorted to, while knowing quite well that I did not really believe it. I was also sufficiently lucid to be able to consider Jacques' behaviour in the light of my own sexual practices, even to the point where my conscience began making a moralistic speech ('What gives you the right to reproach Jacques for something you do yourself?') to a stereotyped version of myself (the unfaithful woman, now herself the victim of infidelity). A stereotype created by my conscience, in exactly the same way as moralizers partly invent the sinners they preach to. Never before had I become so enmeshed in the patterns which our culture imposes on us as though they were simple laws of nature (whether in the form of what we pick up – often simplified – through reading novels or cheap gossip, which is only ever a degenerate version of the same). Sometimes it was deliberate, as in the example with the taxi driver. At other times, the fiction trickled insidiously into my bloodstream. Deep down, I was never remotely tempted to reproach Jacques for his sexual conduct. If there was ever any ill feeling, there were other causes for it, which I will go into later. I was not even afraid that Jacques might bear me a grudge for my frenzied indiscretions. I was acting as a libertine: there existed no higher principle by which to condemn or forbid my actions.

So I was not afraid of guilt, only of the particular kind of suffering which the fruits of my investigations would bring about. And yet! When my investigation yielded nothing, I felt no relief. It did not reassure me at all. Empty-handed, I could think of only one thing: that I would renew my search another time.

If ever my expectations were satisfied, because I had opened an explicit letter, or a new female name had cropped up, the result was an appalling physical sensation: a dry, glacial wave came over my body. Anyone who has ever set out to look for the proof they dread knows this: the moment they fill in what they believe to be the yawning gap of knowledge which is obsessing them, the blood suddenly vanishes from their veins. The proof is actually not a discovery at all, it was already fully, if dimly present in their minds, and it is actualization, the passage from fantasy to reality, which guts them. It is dread – not just of what is real, but also in the face of their own perfect prescience, what alienates them from themselves. They suffer when they find they have been betrayed, and they suffer, also, in the face of the extraordinary power of their intuitions. There seems to be something inhuman about this ability to foresee the improbable, and one's misfortune seems to be all the greater because one failed to prevent it. At such moments, I had a very clear sense of being split down the middle. Because I could not bear to see myself as the woman who had imagined the truth before it came to destroy her, I preferred to look in on her from the outside. My blood, which felt as though it was draining out of me, and my belly, which seemed also as if it might need to empty itself, were forerunners of my spirit, which was also trying to escape. My legs trembled, as though the blood flow which supported them had gone. When I caught hold of my arm, or my hand, it felt as though I was touching something which did not belong to me. Since my body anchored me in a reality which was intolerable, the best thing was to leave it. On several occasions this sensation was so violent that my legs gave way. Whereas at the time the first photographs I had seen on Jacques' desk and my initial reading of the page in his notebook had only provoked a moderate reaction, subsequently the simple verification of what I had extrapolated on the basis of this discovery almost made me faint.

The material was rich. The paleographer dug out the manuscripts and lost herself in deciphering them until the forest of signs closed over her head. The early fragments suggested stories which excited the imagination and made her want to go further. It proved what I knew already, that secret liaisons produce good storylines. A secret frees the imagination, lovers make up for the little time they spend together by complicating the situation, thus convincing themselves of the intensity of their bond. So: her letters and his diaries, between them, supplied the scenario of their first meeting. They scarcely knew each other, but she had asked him to read the manuscript of an erotic story she had written. Then, without revealing his identity, he had arranged a meeting at her flat. He had found the door open, had recognized the layout of her place from the description in her story. When he got to the bedroom he found her wearing only a negligee, ready and waiting, again just like the story. It only remained for me to add detail to this already elaborate canvas.

Other clues left me more scope for invention. Allusions to ordinary details of everyday life put me on the track of a longer-running story. As I had enlarged the field of my investigation, I found the telephone number of L's parents in Jacques' address book. That meant his relationship with the young woman was sufficiently well-established for her family to know about it, and for him to be received into their home, possibly as a son-in-law.

Whenever I came across a meeting with her in his diary, I

went and looked in my own diary to see what I was doing at that time, that day. I pieced together their meetings against a background recollection of my own activities. If Jacques wasn't where I had thought him to be at the very moment when I was busy doing something else, it must mean he had what might be called a double life; picturing myself as I was at that time, ignorant, trusting, I felt an almost physical sense of exclusion from his other life.

I have seen archeologists at work. Using fine pieces of string, they divide up the site into sections of less than a metre square, and each person scratches away at his square with a spoon. Not even a shard of pottery the size of a finger nail escapes their notice. I worked in the same way in the space occupied by Jacques. He is rather messy, and is always leaving crumpled scraps of paper about the house with notes scribbled on them. I have always found this irritating. I've never dared to throw them away in case there is a telephone number on them, or notes he might want again later. Now, I got into the habit of uncrumpling and reading them.

If there was nothing much to be found in the pile of post on the shelf, I would look in the desk drawer. It was here that he kept his photographs, all in a heap. Now, in addition to the names to which I had been able to put a face, because I had occasionally met them, there were also faces and bodies for which I had no names. I examined the negatives by placing them on a white surface. Sometimes I would use a magnifying glass. One series of nudes, from which the head had been cut off, remained a mystery, partly, of course, because there was no way I could identify the person, but also because I wondered whose idea it had been for Jacques to conceal the identity of the model. It was out of character for him. Although I had begun to accept that part of his life was hidden from me, I didn't think that it was hidden from everyone. In fact he was not leading a double life – the proof being the ease with which I was able to discover the traces, the negligence with which he left them within easy reach of my curiosity – he had a life, in the margin of which was his life with me.

I was aware that my inquisitorial determination was bordering on addiction. The symptoms of my addiction were the increasing frequency of my actions, the need for ever greater pain. Before long, the little pieces of paper found by chance were not enough, I would go and look through his pockets for more. I committed two or three acts of petty theft: a sheet from a notepad on which was written, in a woman's handwriting, a mini-dictionary, giving what I took to be Jacques' first name translated into Polish and, if I remember correctly, a few elements of erotic vocabulary; a photograph of a naked woman, which I identified, and which, it seemed, must have been taken a while ago. I did not keep them so as to be able to produce them in front of Jacques and catch him out. I put them with the mess in my own drawers. From time to time I would take them out, even though there was not much else I could glean from one short list of words, or a photograph of a sweetly naked woman in the anonymous decor of a hotel room. Their sole function was to trigger total surrender to grief. Surrender was still the surest way, even though I did not use it consciously, to rid myself of endless conjecture, to put a temporary stop to the conversations with which I badgered Jacques in my imagination, even to forget my intricate plans for vengeance. With tangible evidence in my hands, I could take a bit of a break. Bitter but unambiguous certainty distracted me from dwelling endlessly on my suspicions.

The logic of the investigator is to seek a connection between facts which are not necessarily connected by logic. In accordance with this principle, I embarked on an entirely literal exegesis of Jacques' books. I browsed through them all again and imposed on the vaguest sketch of the figure of a woman, or descriptions of erotic scenes, the flesh and spirit I had accrued by reading the letters and notebooks. I interpreted scenes in settings familiar to me (the garden of Maillol's house in Banyuls, or Carrousel's in Paris) as though they were faithful recordings of reality. Now, although this kind of scrupulous attention to the object may well correspond to the way I describe works in my critical writings, it is far removed from the method used by Jacques, who, as a writer, is no realist! By comparison with the precision assumed in the description of other heroines, C. now seemed to me no more than an abstract symbol, an empty shell.

During the course of my selective and harried re-readings, what caught my eye were the passages in which I thought I recognized places where we often walked together, where he had taken photos of me, where we had made love, or in which I detected allusions to characteristic gestures of mine. I had the technique of the poor student who, skimming through a book, can only identify the passages which will be useful for his dissertation. But these markers soon escaped me. It was as though Jacques' books were printed on blotting paper which soaked up and broke down the symbols which I thought I had recognized. Whenever a figure who could not be me appeared in a setting which belonged to me, whenever a detail differed from my own recollection of the place or events, it was as though my life were being absorbed by the fibrous material and dissolving there. The same procedure applied to the evocation of a body. If he described a back, I imagined it as mine, but not if he described someone's arse. Then my image of myself would disappear into the page, making way for some other woman's image.

Like many people who read novels written in the first person, when I read Jacques' books I always imagined the narrator looking like him, even if the events described were very different to those I believed the author to have experienced. I had never, however, stopped to ask myself whether these novels were to some degree about things which had really happened. I didn't ask myself anything, in fact, since from the outset I had adopted an almost professional attitude with regard to his work. I am not one of those prescriptive critics who place themselves on a level footing with the artist and interfere with the creative process by trying to advise them on their work, or even, on occasions, on their way of life. I confine myself to looking at the result; whether I like it or not, it seems to me that the intellectual or existential grounds from which it proceeds belong to a completely private domain, where the artist, the writer must be completely free of influence. Perhaps I had maintained this sense of distance with Jacques because he himself very rarely opened up about his work and his motivation, and he had never given me any of his novels to read before they came out. There may also be another factor. There was a time, before we really knew each other, when Jacques temporarily had a column in an art magazine and we had found ourselves publicly taking opposite sides in an intellectual argument. This was the origin of a feeling which had persisted between us, that despite all that we shared in our lives, beyond our disagreements, of which there were some, within the privacy of our work we each had our own separate path. This being the case, I didn't even stop to wonder about the character he called C. Of course, I was always pleased to find her there. These little chipped discs, dotted through his books, were little winks and nods which stood out from the great mass of words. But I did not try to work out whether, by use of this sign, Jacques was trying to say something about me, or if need be, tell me something. Only once had I been concerned because the story thrust C. into a series of erotic adventures in Japan and once when I was talking to a Japanese person with whom I worked, they mentioned it in my presence, with a smile. More generally, when an allusion was made clearly to something we had experienced together, or something I had told him about, the only thing I was struck by was the anecdotal aspect, which surprised or amused me. I recall, in particular, being amazed to come across a reference to making love on the bonnet of a car, years after I had told him about it, and long after I had forgotten (suppressed?) the fact that I had told him about it. But I would never have questioned him about why he had chosen one event rather than another. For that, C. would need to stop winking.

drive

The loveliest mosaics, the most exquisite marquetry, have never really been to my taste. Even when they create the effect of space seen in perspective, like the complex marquetry in the *studiolo* of the Ducal Palace in Urbino, where the same elaborately worked surfaces which trap the visitor inside a fake architecture of pilasters and *tablettes* also create the illusion of niches and cupboards filled with books and strange objects to which one's eyes are drawn, as well as of windows through which one would like to gaze out onto the landscape of the plain, I can never entirely forget the fact that they are made up of a large number of small elements fitted tightly together. There is no air between them; I have difficulty in making out the illusory opening in the wall, and the work seems stiff to me, as impermeable as common tiling.

The chimeras that materialized from the depths of Jacques' pockets and drawers were more than a simple background to my onanism, they invaded all the free space in my thoughts. They banished chance, hope, absence of mind, anything which introduces a little playfulness into the mechanism of daily life. Before I lay down in the evening, or rose from my bed in the morning, they got their claws into me; in the street, a passing woman with the slightest resemblance to one of Jacques' women, or even an object in a shop window – a book the two of them had discussed, a piece of jewellery which, on the basis of a quite possibly distorted reading of her character, I imagined to be the kind she might wear – immediately triggered a new episode in the story. And all the time I was just longing to get back to it, looking ahead to moments of passivity in my day. The journeys between home and the office afforded slots of time of adequate length, which they immediately colonized. I neglected my usual reading. I lost all interest in the weary denizens of the metro, whose state of abandon it had, until then, been my pleasure to share. I developed inhibitions, similar to those I spoke of earlier, in connection with masturbation; the presence of other people hampered me. If the stranger on the seat next to me drew themselves to my attention by sneezing, or talking a little loudly, I felt deeply irritated. It interrupted my daydreams, and obliged me to rewind.

It was a while now since I had broken off my sexual relationship with the moody lover I spoke of earlier, and this obsession took the exact place of the reveries I had used to compensate for the rarity of my meetings with him. In contrast to these, however, and to all the shapeless fictions which had served me so well throughout my life, I was no longer the heroine; I was not even the spectator whom the main character is obliged to take account of; I was the extra, ignored and shunned by the lead. I no longer dreamed a dream of my life, I dreamed a dream of Jacques'. I always kept a mild tranquilliser in my bag. When the pain gripped too tight, I surreptitiously slipped a pill onto my tongue and this was enough to relieve the pressure. There was something in me of the alcoholic, who, with the best will in the world, claims she only drinks a glass with meals, when she has carefully placed a reserve of bottles in various hiding places, behind old piles of laundry or disused crockery. What motive would I have had for getting well, when it was this same obsession which both saturated my imagination *and* offered the only possible prospect of an opening, the one which looked out over that vast plain, the unreclaimed territory of Jacques' life?

I had enough information to be able to imagine Jacques in all sorts of different circumstances, besides erotic episodes: journeys which I certainly knew about, but had not realized had both an ostensible and a secondary purpose (that of spending a few days in the company of a woman), dinners, parties he had attended with one or another of them, at the houses of friends I knew well, or of people I did not know, and whom I did not even realize he knew, all of which spread out around him a network of activities and relationships to which I had no physical access, so that every gesture, word or habit of his began to radiate out infinite possibilities, both banal and mysterious, which I immediately set about reconstructing. On two or three occasions, Jacques, who, unlike me, is not possessed of an exact memory, tried to get me to remember a party I never went to, convinced that it was I who had been with him. If I had really thought about it, I could have taken some consolation from the fact that my shadow had eclipsed another woman in his memory. But it was the other explanation which immediately suggested itself to me. Our past life together was like a vast airbag which was now beginning to deflate and Jacques' mistake opened up a minuscule valve through which a little more of the air we had breathed together was expelled.

I should add that in some hidden recess of my body I felt the valve tighten again, once the bubble had passed.

From then on it was like living in a cage from which I could see Jacques coming and going, and sporadically vanishing off the horizon, without being able to join him and share the same space with him. Whenever he answered the telephone, and began talking, while moving away from me, being careful to say immediately: 'Ah! Hello! I'm just here with Catherine, we're…', or hanging up sharply, cursing a wrong number, not only did I feel quite sure that one of his girlfriends was trying to get hold of him, but also, on the basis of a couple of words picked up by my ever alert ears, I immediately came up with a precise identity and physical presence. This spontaneous vision was actually pretty much always the same composite, a fusion of different models taken from vague memories, if I had seen them before, in real life or in a photo, or if I had read a description of their body by Jacques: a youthful-looking girl, rather large, with light brown hair… As when I had rummaged in his bureau, I became short of breath and my heart briefly began to race.

The cage closed in. One day, Blandine came to our house to shoot some scenes as part of a little film she was making; she needed an interior like ours, and she needed Jacques to take part. I shut myself up in what was then my tiny office, in order to work. Suddenly, Jacques popped his head round the door to ask me to join them, and perhaps feed them a few lines. This suggestion seemed to me unbelievably cruel. I was prepared to open the door to Blandine, say hello to her, but I was not going to enter the room she was jointly occupying with Jacques, as though he was still living in the little studio he had back in the now distant days when we revealed ourselves to each other for the first time, in which three people could not have fitted comfortably. I feared that I might find myself hurtling into my nightmare world. I knew neither of them was likely to treat me ambivalently, or make me feel awkward; with hindsight, I suppose it may have been that the danger of attaching my flights of fancy onto real people really terrified me. Who knows, I might have found myself pushing them onto the sofa in an attempt to set in motion the sexual encounter I had endlessly fantasized about, before leaving the room, implicitly driven from it, as imagined in one of my scenarios. After all, in the past I had been quite accustomed to such situations, quite able, for example, in more or less impromptu orgies, to play the apprentice madame, leading a woman to a man. On several occasions, I had played this game with Jacques, initiating a *ménage à trois* with one of my friends; these were, moreover, the very few occasions when I had not been able to sustain my role till the end, and had ended up by becoming aggressive. Would I, in this case, have set up the scene and then, instead of melodramatically relishing my eviction, found my fantasy ending like these feeble other attempts, in abysmal failure? More likely, nothing at all would have happened, in which case another obligation would have presented itself, that of abandoning my fantasies and fitting in with the paradoxical reality in which there was no pretence: Jacques and Blandine would have modified their behaviour in light of my presence and I myself would hypocritically have behaved as though I suspected nothing. Sometimes, when we wake up from a bad dream, we hesitate before opening our eyes, not out of fear that the dream will continue, but, on the contrary, out of fear of leaving it, because deep down we are reluctant to leave the cocoon in which suffering is held in check, preferring to keep it in a semi-conscious realm for as long as possible, because in some secret place even deeper in our psyche we know that it is inescapable anyway. Obviously I hadn't thought all this out clearly when I reacted to Jacques' suggestion with a look of dumb horror, which irritated him. And there I stayed, alone, staring at my computer.

Jacques and his theory of ghosts gradually took over every-thing, so that I could scarcely even find room for the aura of my own body. If I found hairs inside my motorbike helmet, which, from their length, I knew weren't mine, I simply could not wear the helmet again. I found myself thereafter going through the automatic procedures for opening the garage door when we came back from a ride – turning the key, opening the first shutter, raising the catch hooked into the ground, reach-ing up on tiptoe to pull down the one at the top, while holding the second shutter in place, and finally opening this shutter wide to allow the motorbike room to pass through – while slipping inside the silhouette of another woman, who, I was quite sure, must have had to learn the same series of move-ments when she had stayed at the house. Even today it is not unusual, when I go through these movements, for me to perform them like a drama student, who copies as exactly as possible the attitudes the teacher has just shown her, or even stands behind him so as to produce an immediate replica, like a shadow. Even the bathroom became occupied territory. Some time back, Jacques had asked me to be careful to sponge the edge of the bathtub after my shower, because he was worried that the water might seep into the wall. I had always carefully, mechanically repeated the gesture, until one fine day, it occurred to me to wonder whether the same recommendation had been made to other women who happened to use the bathroom, and whether they complied. From that day forward, every time I finished in the bathroom, I repeated this gesture, but this time it was accompanied, or rather preceded by the gesture of another woman. The result was several minutes of prostration. Absorbed by this image, I could no longer instruct my body to move and sometimes, when I had to simply give up altogether, I could not hold back the tears. Tears often flowed, too, when I saw my own reflection in a small mounted mirror which I used for putting on and taking off my makeup. I had great difficulty looking at my face, finding myself in a state of confusion, overwhelmed both by the kind of guilty nostalgia you feel when, coming across a portrait of someone you were very fond of, who has now died, you give it a surreptitious glance, preferring not to be reminded of the degree to which you have forgotten their face, and by an oppressive sense of shame, because I could not help but see the haggard face which looked back at me as that of a poor neurotic woman. For the ability to stand back from myself never left me completely, even in my worst moments. My eyes stared into those other eyes, emptied of all expression by the simultaneous, but conflicting effects of pity and disgust, and I am quite sure I did not see the edges of my face.

The little fictions I invented to trigger my solitary pleasure were the first clear proof that my imagination had been taken prisoner. Curiously, in this realm, that of immediate pleasure, I did struggle to regain my freedom to fantasize. Often I would start to caress myself, deliberately drawing on an image from my old portfolio, but try as I might, the most familiar stories no longer got me sufficiently excited, at which point, in a rage, fully conscious of my foolish subordination, I would call up one or other of the scenes played out by Jacques and one of his girlfriends. I tried to keep a clear sense of how long I had been languishing down in the barren depths of my imagination. If I had been able to mark the days on the walls of my imaginary cell, I would have done it; I counted months, then years, never knowing whether I would one day be reunited with myself in what has to be the ultimate solo sex act.

I did not demonstrate the same – admittedly useless – degree of perceptiveness in the many other spheres of my symbolic world which I found being progressively taken from me. In this symbolic world, the village of Illiers-Combray, which Jacques knew well, as he had spent his childhood near there, was a great intersection of meanings and emotions. We had been there several times, the first time with his parents, and then with close friends; with the help of one of these friends we had taken a photo showing our silhouettes, which had been intended for use as the cover for one of Jacques' books. He and I had posed on the lawn of a small hotel, bearing the enigmatic name – how could we have failed to notice – 'Hotel de L'Image'. I should add that I had read *In Remembrance of Things Past* and begun to love Proust during the first summer we spent together. There is a river flowing through us, lapping round our emotions, depositing the sediment of memory, and the waters of this river brought together the reactions I had had on reading the narrator's account of his childhood memories, others which came from the subjective novel I had been inventing from hearing Jacques talk about his own childhood, and impressions simply of our life together, for which the markers were already being laid down, slight in themselves, but heavy with emotion. Now, not only had Jacques made the same excursion together with L., they had even taken a room at an inn called the Moulin de Montjouvin. Had I not also been secretly planning just such an escapade for the two of us? The discovery that they had headed me off took me by surprise while I was still waiting for the right moment to suggest it. The image evoked by the page of the notebook in which I found out about it was that of a charming country inn transformed into an ironic cliché in this everyday tale of adultery. It thrust itself upon me, pervaded by the famous passage in which the girlfriend of Mademoiselle Vinteuil, wrapping her arms around her, teases her into a perverted game, threatening to spit on the portrait of her dead father, a scene Proust sets in the father's house, which he names Montjouvain. Even the first time I read it, the description of this behaviour had made such a striking and profound impression on me that I had gone back to read it again, wondering whether I had understood it properly, or whether I might not be guilty of too personal an interpretation. In what later became one of my fiercest fantasies, I did not go so far as to reproduce the scene identically, I subverted it into a gross and outrageous act: I firmly anchored Jacques to the backside of the young woman on all fours on a bed, in broad daylight, with the bedroom window open onto a park, and contented myself with having him say, as he brutally shoved her arse back and forward, with the determination of someone struggling with a stubborn drawer in a dresser, that no woman had ever made him come like she did. That was sufficient self-abasement, and the spectacle stopped there. I took care to inflict on myself just the right degree of pain, as enthusiasts of sado-masochism hover just on the threshold of what the body can bear without breaking, so as not to jeopardize the further pursuit of pleasure. To have her spit on a photograph of me would have perhaps been so intolerable that I would have had to break off my dream. Perhaps I was only prepared to grant myself a masochistic thrill on condition that it be filtered through this kind of quasi-burlesque representation, just as Mademoiselle Vinteuil, who, for Proust, is not without virtue, can only allow herself to take pleasure when she is pretending to be 'bad'.

Other superimpositions were even more disturbing. Years before this, we had been riding along a mountain road on the motorbike, when we saw down below us a couple who were bathing naked in a stream, tourists probably, and for the brief duration of the vision, we were amused by it, and remarked admiringly on the woman's body, which was tall and athletic. It was such a lovely scene, like one from classical antiquity, that it made a lasting impression on me, even though there was nothing about it in particular which drew me, I had no particular fondness for the place, and Jacques and I did not find reason to revisit the incident at a later date. Now I believed I had come across this identical story in Jacques' diary, but now in the form of a little escapade of which a certain Dany and he were the protagonists. He had set it in exactly the same spot, on the road to Serrabonne. It was very hot, he had stopped the bike and they had climbed down to the stream and bathed completely naked in the 'freezing water'. Have I now embroidered on what I read? I seem to think that the episode ended in a bucolic coitus. I can offer no explanation for the disconcerting displacement of an event that Jacques and I witnessed as spectators, into the realm of his life without me. Had the sight of the bathers made an impression on him also, so much so that he later wished to imitate them? Or had I invented a false memory, based on Jacques' story? Or had he come up with a fantasy which mingled memory and desire? Thus, events which in my brain were filed as memories were transformed into premonitions of events in the part of Jacques' life in which I did not figure. In earlier times, I would have been thought to be under a spell, like the butcher in the story, who, in his impulsiveness, ends up with nothing but a string of sausages hanging from his nose: no sooner had I summoned up a mental image, however innocent, the memory of a walk we had taken on holiday, for instance, than it would be transformed into an act committed by Jacques, adding fuel to the black thoughts swarming in my brain.

It was like saying Hail Marys to the devil: I thumbed through the rosary of normal thoughts, and at regular intervals, the conjunction of some circumstance of everyday life and an episode – frequently one no less anodyne – from Jacques' other life, would reveal a poignant insight into which I would enter like a mystic upon the state of ecstasy. We might be discussing picking up a friend from the train station. I would find myself imagining him meeting a different friend, and in my mind's eye I watched him as he relieved her of her suitcase and kissed her on the corner of her lips. My spy glass was focused in such a way that, just as in the masturbatory fantasies I concentrated principally on the position of Jacques' body and his face, all I saw here was his face moving towards a phosphene. He might suggest we take a walk; I would panic, as though, having set out alone, I would be bound to meet them on my way, and be torn between fleeing, hiding, or walking on past. This occurred so frequently that I ended up living part of the time alongside a man who was essentially the product of my imagination, and, despite everything, a stranger, who literally fascinated me. With my inner eye, I watched him night and day. It was a waking dream, but, just as in night dreams we are sometimes drawn to an object which we cannot reach, as though we were bogged down in something sticky, in the same way, I could not reach this Jacques, all of which only stirred my curiosity and increased my distress.

This other life of Jacques, which I had dreamed up, was an Eden, in which he appeared to find pleasure without reservation, without guilt, without resentment, in the complete absence of any emotional or moral authority to justify or judge him, completely unaware of my existence. His various manoeuvres had an arbitrary quality, whose logic was to me, as a non-initiate, entirely enigmatic. His character was smooth. Even when he was dissimulating, lying, deceiving, the account provided no psychological explanation (that Jacques might have been seeking to punish me, or avenge some offence I had committed against him), it was as though it was all part of some transcendent mechanism. My astonishment reminded me of nothing so much as the feeling I had as a child when I was told about the commandments imposed on men by the ancient gods, without their being given any explanation of the reasons behind them. I had made Jacques into a myth.

I dug out the letters he had sent me at the beginning of our relationship and which I read at the time in great haste; now I underlined passages with a red pen. How could I reconcile the Jacques who said that love was 'incompatible with the nature of shared domesticity' and 'made it impossible to launch into the cycle of petty acts of cowardice and compromises', and the

Jacques who had reorganized his time without my realizing, filling it with events without my knowledge? Or that by opening them up to other people he had transformed our homes into places which would now feel to me more like his than mine; or that the walks we had discovered together and which we repeated might now remind him of pleasures which I had not been part of and which his rather unreliable memory might mix up with our own? And having written 'The only lies are sexual lies. Morality is only ever sexual. Let there be no lies between us, no concealment, if the truth is perverted things will always come to light and end in catastrophe', how had he justified those absences, the reason for which was kept from me? I could not, unaided, fit them together. I had no argument with the content of the letters, which, when they first arrived, I had told myself I would try to understand fully another time, and which continued to declare supernatural truths I was not yet mature enough to grasp. And my confidence in Jacques was, at the same time, too deep-rooted for me to suspect him of cynicism at the time of writing or, later, of inconsistency or betrayal. Absurdly, and yet sincerely, I was waiting for Jacques to find a way of making his account of his relationship with his girlfriends fit in with the logic of the arguments he had used then. I called endlessly for explanations. Face to face over dinner, lying side by side in the middle of the night, on the phone while Jacques was in the house in the Midi and I was in Paris, sometimes on the basis of a letter one of us had written to the other, during sessions which could last for hours, we talked. Sometimes we debated calmly, but more often, because I needed to rediscover his *whole* personality, I acted liked a spinning compass. I started by shaking my head from right to left, or by waving my hands around, then came my whole body, and then the sobs which empty out the body. We called this 'the crises'. And we refer to the period throughout which they continued, almost three years, as 'the crisis'.

Each time the crisis took exactly the same course. Either my spying had brought to light a new detail in Jacques' mythical life, or, as in the case above, a tiny incident brutally reminded me of an episode or a person. In either case, I experienced it like a hallucination. There you are, working, your ideas flowing. Then, all of a sudden, in the mind's eye a photograph interrupts your thinking and your attention is diverted towards a phantom woman, resting her elbows on a balustrade overlooking the sea, her hair escaping from a scarf which is coming loose. You dismiss the vision, you reread the phrase left hanging on the computer screen, but then focus again on the balustrade, in an attempt to identify the place, it's a balustrade of the pseudo-antique kind you find in tasteful, and somewhat pretentious hotels. You tell yourself you'll go and look at the photograph again a bit later, just to clear things up. Without pause, you move on, of course, to the elegant, generously cut coat enveloping the woman, the true focus of your obsession, the carefully wielded instrument of torture, glowing red-hot in the black and white image. There are times during which work has much less pull on the imagination than what we erroneously call 'distractions' – at such times my intellectual activity progressed only sporadically, in segments which had managed to escape the influence of these phantasms.

. . . . .

Although I never considered conducting my investigations
into Jacques' mythical life other than alone – I would never
have asked the subject of them to explain himself freely, I
needed this laborious, clandestine solitude too much, just as I
needed to get close to the material evidence, which his sense
of decency would have stopped him showing me – bizarrely, I
also had no wish to come out with them in such a way as to
embarrass him, or seem to be accusing him. Even at the beginning, without thinking about it, I had kept my discoveries
secret, in the hope that he would see and understand the stig-
mata they left upon me; I was waiting for him to volunteer to
tend them, I wanted proof of a love which was so perfect that
Jacques would be able to feel what I was feeling myself
telepathically. The untranslatable imperative was that his
response would only be worth anything if it came before I
asked for it. As a result I spent a great deal of time taking some
mortifying scenario and mentally tacking on another one in
which Jacques consoled me, proving that he knew me so well,
that my grief was so guileless (and it was true to say that
having, up to that point, suspected nothing, I was not prepared for it and had therefore developed no resistance) that he
could immediately, by intuition, guess what had caused it. Parallel to the fantasies in which I had him treat me with pure con-
tempt, that is to say, in which he totally ignored me, I
developed others in which, on the contrary, he showed an
almost miraculous sensitivity in his concern for me, a saint-like
receptivity. Through the very act of helping me heal my
wounds, Jacques would have reunited the two aspects of
himself. In other words, I had a long wait ahead!

Happy are the poor of imagination! Happy are those who can read the signs clearly, without going and plunging into Talmud and the Massorah, those who act without worrying about all of their actions' possible consequences and envisioning in advance the response to each one, who do not try to reweave the past and are not superstitious, those who do not talk to themselves in the voice of those who would gainsay them... How many times had Jacques reproached me for not being satisfied with the present? I could have told him that my endless dialogues with him expanded the present for, somewhere deep inside me, they never stopped; he would then be surprised, because he had already forgotten the previous row, while I carried on arguing in silence, and had finally thought of the correct response to one of his observations. I prepared my phrases as though I were going to have to pronounce them in public, shaping them in advance, so judicious in my use of words that sometimes I would go and check their meaning in the dictionary. In general it was a waste of time; since, obviously, having missed my inner reasoning, Jacques pointed out that I was talking in riddles. And so I improvised, and, struggling with the wrong words, I sank deeper still into the shifting sands of mutual incomprehension.

I invented countless strategies for letting him know, without actually telling him, that the photo (which he himself might have been astonished to find buried at the back of a drawer where his hand scarcely ever strayed) had come to my attention, and that all I was asking for, in fact, was a little more information about who it was, the approximate date when it had been taken, and exactly where it had been taken, how long the relationship had lasted, just the straight facts. If I thought I recognized the place, then I lost no opportunity to refer to it, as though Jacques might then take the opportunity to talk to me about the woman he had taken there. Or I might suggest to him that he preferred girls with long hair, rather than short, like mine. If he had been crazy enough to say that yes of course, there was nothing he found more sensual than running his hands through the hair of the woman in question, whose name was Françoise, and with whom – fancy that! – he had ridden down the road I knew so well myself – I would surely have experienced the very same delicious pain to which my own fantasies led me, the confirmation of my exclusion. I thought I knew roughly when the photo had been taken. My detours could get even more tortuous; I began to mention the difficulties I had had around that time, how much moral support I had needed, and I waited dumbly for Jacques to feel guilty and confess the reason why he had not noticed my distress. None of which he did, of course, and having put off my own confession as long as possible, I would suddenly blurt out, exhausted by my tête-à-tête with the apparition in the photo: 'I found a photo at the back of the drawer.'

One of the good things about dreams is that, however terrible the atrocities we commit in them, or however indecently we behave, we are never punished. I was so immersed in the atmosphere of my obsession that at first I did not see how bruised Jacques felt by my appropriation of his private papers, and by my hermeneutics in interpreting his books. What it amounted to, in the end, was a kind of rummaging about in his unconscious. It wasn't until he wrote to me describing the damage caused by my intrusion into what he held most precious (that and our life together) – his writing, and the fantasy games which fuelled it, as he put it, until he spelled out in large letters the extent to which he felt 'emptied and defeated' that I began to realize. Until then, I had never doubted that the man who saw right to the heart of me would explain all, and forgive all.

An obsession could keep me tight-lipped for several days, stop me accepting an invitation (from people Jacques had spent time with in the company of one of his mysterious partners), or avoiding using an object (because she had touched it); I lived like an invalid, whose feeble gestures are confined to the limits of her sickbed, numbed, trussed up by a host of taboos, all of which must have been quite incomprehensible to Jacques, who watched me, and recognized, with some apprehension, all the signs of an impending crisis. In general, when I finally expressed myself explicitly, in a single sentence, with a tremendous sigh, as though I had just made a huge physical effort, looking off into the distance, because just at that moment I was no more than a particle hanging in suspension, Jacques' reply was immediate. Not once did he give me an answer, at least, not the one I was looking for. He pointed out my own behaviour, the fact that I had never stopped going to orgies and that, above all, for long periods I had desired other people, not him. And it is true that while I was busy counting and examining his relationships with women, he was busy updating the list of my lovers. I had learned from reading his diaries that he had suspected some of them, but the method I had unthinkingly adopted automatically meant I couldn't discuss them with him. The decent thing to do would have been to place our disclosures on an equal footing, to have spoken first, and then asked him to do the same. But as I have explained, I was waiting first for him to 'infer' my unasked questions, and respond to them spontaneously, and sometimes, not out of honesty, but to lead him indirectly to confide in me,

I would decide to tell him I had had a sexual relationship with so and so, usually confirming an existing suspicion. I would throw out some ballast, in the hope of advancing a little further into his world.

Assessing the negative balance – 'what you never told me, what you never understood, what I could never tell you, where we failed…' – is the game which couples in conflict always play but which no one can win. They do not realize that the line dividing the two sides of their balance sheet is also a joining line. Whatever the outcome of their dispute, whether or not the couple survives, the moments, the actions in which the partners believed they acted separately constitute a zone which, although not clearly defined, has a zigzag of stitches running through it. It is like the comings and goings of farce. A character enters stage left just as the person he is looking for exits stage right, there is a partition between them, but where necessary, a voice, or a glance, or a misunderstanding may pass from one side to the other. On odd occasions in the past, I had stumbled across clues to the hidden parts of Jacques' life. As I have said: they did not strike me at the time and it was only now that I began to see them clearly. One such clue was a gesture I had seen Jacques make towards one of his female friends. He had written a play which was being performed out of Paris and his friends had hired a coach, so we could go to the opening night. There were a lot of us, and the trip, including the return journey to Paris, late at night, was full of gaiety. We arrived back, and by the dim light of the streetlamps in the Place de la Nation, I saw Jacques stroke the cheek of a young woman asleep at the rear of the coach with the back of his index finger. I recognized the gesture with which he had touched me the first time we met. I had myself travelled the whole way next to F., one of my friend–lovers, and we had spent the entire trip working ourselves up in an amiable discussion of aesthetics. The next day, in his diary, Jacques had written: 'Doubts about Catherine. Affair with F.?' I myself had not written anything, I had witnessed the scene, I had interpreted it on the spot, and immediately put it to the very back of my mind, with no more soul-searching than if the back window of the coach had been a cinema screen. But now I retrieved it, and in the narrow interior of the coach, with its low roof, under which the occupants had to move around leaning forwards across each other, in an attitude akin to one of protection or tenderness, our gestures, our words, both mine and Jacques', as well as those with which others addressed us, acquired substance and intersected, grazing each of the four of us as they flew amongst us like bats. The farce developed into a strange, suspended kind of foursome, in which our attitudes, our utterances, as well as our glances, which reveal the desires and feelings which exist between people, without necessarily articulating them, circulated among us.

We can no more choose the mistress or lover of the man or woman we love than we can our family, or theirs, and the kind of sexual proximity we are suddenly thrust into by certain revelations may sometimes feel like an involuntary surrender of principle, or even a tainting of the self, a corruption of our own capacity for physical love. Since from very early on I had left many of my sexual encounters to chance, and had as a result learned not to be too fussy in this area, I am sure I found this kind of intimacy less bruising than Jacques did. He, on the other hand, found himself faced by a disparate range of representatives of humanity, whose company he did not always find flattering. I saw him pass from dejection to disgust, and even to downright indignation when I confirmed that I had indeed slept with someone he found completely ridiculous, someone he had identified as a troublemaker or one of his friends whom he felt had behaved improperly. I can remember exactly the position of our bodies and the look on his face when I pronounced certain names, lowering my voice, and using the almost-interrogative form you adopt when you introduce a topic of conversation by just making sure that the person you are talking to knows the person in question: 'You know who I mean? You remember So-and-so?' On one occasion especially, when we were standing on the little landing outside the bedroom, he at the foot of the stairs which lead up to the next floor, and I on the threshold of the bedroom, with one foot already in it, I had caught sight of the look on his face, combining all these feelings. It was like when I was preparing to leave the apartment I shared with Claude, an event of which I have retained only the visual memory of my suitcase lying open on the bed, on this occasion too, my visual perception must have been functioning to perfection, for the image it was fixed on has pushed out any other images and thoughts which would have been intolerable, such as a lustful memory evoked by the name in question, which I had repressed as though Jacques might have been able to see it hanging like some obscene banner above my head. And perhaps I needed this encounter with Jacques to leave a reliable and enduring impression on me, so that when the time came, it would be possible to analyse it?

All the same, when Jacques parried my pressing questions with reminders of my own behaviour, I was completely dumbstruck, as though he had suddenly mistaken me for someone else, and it was only by summoning up all my reason that I managed to avoid considering his remarks unjust. Surely he understood that I had paraded my body about in a carefree, at times almost negligent manner? That I had acted like a true sailor, who hears the call of the ocean and in whose simple mind ports of call drift back to join that vague territory where memories eventually merge with dreams. My life was so compartmentalized and all my sexual relations, whether long-term or impromptu, were so carefully wrapped in the products of my imagination that, in the end, paradoxically, it was not the vagaries of the flesh which connected me to the real world, but rather my life which like a gathering wave had swept my body off into adventures. If anyone had asked me I would have said that my one true link with the real world was the bond I had made long ago with Jacques. This sense of partnership was consolidated by my feeling that none of my adventures had ever affected either my professional life, or my life with him, that I had never imagined we might split up, and that this was the only reality which mattered.

As Jacques pointed out, my sexual system had undoubtedly done much to weaken our own bond, but perhaps in a less mechanical way than it might seem. It was not really my peregrinations which dulled my enthusiasm for Jacques, but rather a slow, general transformation in my behaviour. A casual remark I had made some time before came back to me now. We had not been living together very long. We had gone on a walk with a couple of friends. I can't now recall the subject of our conversation, which was very relaxed – sex, probably, because all of a sudden I exclaimed: 'Jacques chose me because he thought I was obsessed with sex, ah, how wrong can you be!' I said it as a joke, our friends, who were no doubt familiar with my lifestyle, did not appear to take me seriously, and I myself, had I stopped to think about it, would have wondered what could possibly have made me say such a thing, since I didn't believe it for a moment; while I was not strictly speaking 'obsessed with sex', I was still widely available and therefore more active than others in this field. However, not only had I said the words, but I had remembered saying them, even though they were meant as a joke. Was I perhaps already very dimly aware that my libido was in fact somehow changing? I have described how I came to terms with the injunctions in Jacques' early letters to me, and how I minimized my guilt, the natural outcome of my deceit, by making out that the person having these adventures was the bit of me left over from an epoch which pre-dated our relationship. And the fact that I could refer to a Catherine of 'before', meant there must be a present Catherine who was beginning to regard her libertarian philosophy – though libertarian is perhaps too strong a word – with a certain detachment. I no longer had the same reasons for defending her as I had had at the time I wrote that rather exalted letter to Jacques, sitting alone in his flat, reeling from the very first discovery that he occasionally invited another woman there. I was now much more committed to my work. The recognition it brought me went a long way towards satisfying my narcissism; since I felt genuinely free, I perhaps had less need to be a suffragette in the cause of libertarianism. And this increasing distance not only put some distance between me and my various affairs, it also altered the whole nature of my libido. In an old letter, Jacques, quoting Lacan – 'There is no such thing as a sexual relationship' – had accused me of 'believing' in the possibility of sexual relationships. If it is indeed true that I did believe in them at the time Jacques sent this letter, I certainly lost my faith during the period of crisis I am describing now.

How shall I sum up a situation which evolved over fifteen years? You lose touch with a friend, you mean to phone him, and then forget. A different friend, with whom you have spent steamy nights of pleasure, reappears and this time, after a dinner during which there was definitely a certain something in the air, you say goodbye in the taxi with a simple kiss. You don't slide your lips around, nor does he. Another evening you extract yourself from the hydra with four – or maybe more – heads, as it humps and rolls on the big broad bed, and you hear yourself for the first time in your life tell the man trying to stroke you and stop you from leaving that you're really rather tired. I have never got angry, or ended a relationship, never taken any decision which would have changed the direction of my sex life, and I spent very little time dwelling on such small details, knowing I could always drop back easily into my old ways and decide, another time, to prolong the embrace and wave aside my tiredness. But at such times I was like a bad actor who has rehearsed a scene so often, he has lost touch with the part.

My liaison with Jacques had begun in the context of my own particular sexual routine at the time we met, which had since changed, and it seems to me now that our relationship evolved as it did because I tacitly abandoned this routine. At any rate, I chose not to recall that it had once been part of it. Perhaps my strange habit of systematically excluding myself from Jacques' life worked retrospectively so I had begun to apply it in fact to our past relations? I was so busy brooding on my fantasies, in which I pictured him in endless bacchanals with other women, I had become incapable of recalling the times I myself had spent with him. Perhaps I had picked up on something, a long time back, when he criticized my behaviour in one of his letters, and a scruple now told me to avoid 'compromising' my relationship with him, by keeping it separate from this routine. Perhaps I was protecting myself against an insidious kind of guilt, by idealizing our relationship, keeping it at a distance from a coarser kind of sexual exchange. Perhaps in the heat of our discussions, I accepted Jacques' analyses and identified so closely with the picture he seemed to be painting of me, of a girl who was so hooked on multiple and indiscriminate relationships that I could no longer imagine that I had ever found pleasure in the long-term relationship I had with him. Although in our endless discussions we were forever re-examining the tiniest details of our past, I was hit with amnesia when it came to any moment of sexual pleasure I shared with Jacques. He was intent on preserving them; I was concerned to find no trace of them in my normally excellent memory.

I received several postcards, on the back of which he described scenes which he hoped might bring back memories. How once, in a box room, I had sucked his member at length, crouched down, 'with your bare butt sticking out, and your skirt hitched up', before hastily pulling it down to go and greet a visitor, while he remained hidden, with his 'eyes still glued to your arse' bobbing about under the fabric. Another time he described at length the many nights when we did not sleep, when he took me 'in every imaginable position', so he insisted, and I urged him on with my cries, my obscenities, driving my heels into his backside and thighs. I experienced an intense emotion on reading these lines, an emotion in which it was hard to distinguish relief at what I could not but interpret as demonstrations of love – after my obsessive insistence on Jacques' indifference and physical rejection of me – from sexual arousal: each sent the same liberating wave through my body, from solar plexus to vagina. I never tired of his accounts. Their effect was as sharp as if we had really just replayed these scenes, or had just played them out for the very first time.

The postcards arrived when we were apart for several days at a time. We made up for the geographical distance with telephone conversations which left me with an aching ear from pressing the receiver against it. These conversations were terrible. It is not possible, on the telephone, to replace a harsh word with a simple look or, seeing the other's expression, to bite back a cruel retort; so one's remarks are more abrupt, even if the invisibility of the person one is speaking to may, as in the confessional, make it easier to say the really difficult things. We ended up exhausted, having run out of arguments; once I had a slight dizzy spell, which made me drop the phone. Over the next few days I spent my time constructing a new fable in which I didn't really believe, but which at least distracted me from my suffering, relieving it like a placebo: as our conflict was not getting us anywhere, I would initiate our separation myself: I would go and live somewhere else. Along came more questions: I needed my library, how could I fit so many books into a small apartment, and who would keep the cat…? At last, after several hours, or several days, one or the other of us would make the move to pick up the phone, calmly asking something quite banal. Cautiously, we would venture a few words of remission, and as we could not just sink into a silent, comforting embrace, Jacques had come up with the idea of the postcards, which reached me in clusters of four or five. Our bodies were refreshed by their tender pornographic messages, which helped us forget our disembodied conversations. I watched out for them in the post and read and reread them with deep pleasure.

They alienated me deliciously from myself. Since I did not remember the incidents they referred to, each one offered a new opportunity to project myself into Jacques' paradise, from which I believed I was excluded. In my own way, I found this feeling of otherness, which necessarily brought with it a sense of freedom – the freedom to be someone else, freedom to escape, if only for a moment, from suffering – in certain precise circumstances. At the end of our separation, we would meet again. For ten days, maybe two weeks, my solitude had been haunted by dreams, some of which were torture, others con-solation. Whenever Jacques came to meet me at Perpignan airport, or when he was returning to Paris, I availed myself of the first few minutes, an intermediary moment during which we were no longer apart, but had not yet resumed the normal course of shared domesticity, to prolong the dream atmosphere in which I had recently been immersed. Now I could actually experience moments as wonderful as those evoked on the back of the postcards. The scruples I would have had shortly after an argument, and the awkwardness, verging on shyness, I would have felt if we had actually had sex, were overcome. I had travelled wearing nothing under my skirt, and as soon I was sitting next to him in the 4 by 4 he had left in the car park, I rubbed my knee against his, invitingly, so he would place his hand on my thigh, then, by slight movements of my thigh, encouraged him to slide his hand up further, till he discovered the surprise of my exposed pubis. As soon as we were on the road I would start taking off my clothes; I would manage to extract his sex from the tight sheath of his jeans. The effect was intoxicating, utterly liberating. The sensation of speed, which creates the sense that stationary objects by the roadside are being jettisoned in one's wake, creates a specific space around my body, a narrow lawless enclave in which nudity is an animal state, without shame.

Or else, without warning, I would come to meet Jacques at the Gare de Lyon, completely naked under my raincoat. As I walked along beside him on the platform, or sat close to him on the metro, I got a thrill from knowing he had no idea that an object of desire was within touching distance, as one might tease a child who must find the present one has hidden, encouraging him by saying 'You're getting warmer!'; I would be particularly affectionate towards him. I was elated by the thought that in the pressing throng, a mere millimetre's thickness of fabric lay between him and my naked flesh, that a single movement would have sufficed to remove it, as remove it I did, by undoing the belt, just before we passed through the front door of the house. Sometimes we had sex on the doorstep itself.

Although Jacques always brought our arguments right back to questions of sex (my behaviour in general, and with him in particular, which partly explained his own, since, while lately I had seemed 'indifferent' or 'bored', his desire for me had remained intact), and although the fictions I wove around him were as narrowly focused on sexual acts as the camera in a pornographic film, my interrogation of him, my grievances against him, never had any bearing on these acts. Paradoxically, I could imagine him assuring a complete stranger that no woman had ever, in his entire life, given him so much pleasure, and keep the scene playing right to the point of total surrender of his body to orgasm, but I would never have said to him: 'You desired another woman more than me', or, worse still: 'I'm angry because you made love with other women.' This wasn't even because, having reasoned with myself, I had to accept that his freedom was as legitimate as my own; it was because I did not doubt his expressions of love for me, nor the fact that he was sexually very attached to me. In a mood of optimism, I would interrogate him over and over, trusting precisely in his infinite patience, the inexhaustible kindness he showed in his love for me. First, as I have said, I would ask modestly for information regarding the date, the place, or organizational details, at least, this was how I presented it. Although my intention was not entirely clear to me, I was trying to replace each detail of my imaginary reconstruction with its true equivalent, to the best of Jacques' recollection, I wanted to glimpse the hypothetical model of a picture I had already drawn with my eyes closed. However, on the rare occasions when Jacques did respond with some concrete details, this model did not in fact take the place of the imaginary picture, it simply made it possible for me to add in a few more colourful details, which rendered it all the more poignant. I would have liked to have had access to his entire set of diaries over the years, his hour by hour schedule, and a recording of all his engagements. I was trying to climb out of the pool of blood-sucking leeches, I wanted to get back to the man with the clear conscience, living in his carefree world.

After much hesitation, I ventured a first question, formulated as simply and briefly as possible: 'Did you go to dinner at the X's with L.?' I had scarcely finished my sentence when

Jacques immediately reacted with an angry interjection. He had had enough of my 'masochistic jealousy', my 'morbid harping'. I warily pointed to the strictly anodyne nature of my approach: if he would just confirm it I would let it drop. But Jacques had stopped listening to me, he had suffered too, he was suffering even now, and he was the one now asking for mercy. I was defeated. The man who said this was not going to open the gates of his Eden to me, and now all I could do was try, in turn, to make him feel sorry for me, using arguments which ran roughly like this: by principally surrounding himself with very young women he was stigmatizing my body, which was the body of a mature woman; he paid them a kind of paternal attention which I was deprived of; our friends colluded in keeping his affairs secret from me, which made me look ridiculous in their eyes.

During one of the first conversations we had after I had read his diary, I was surprised to find myself telling him, as though on a whim, that if I was going to have to compete with twenty-year-old rivals I had better try cosmetic surgery. The idea had never occurred to me before (and in fact never would again). While expressing this surprising idea, I felt myself adopting the behaviour, and, almost, the appearance, of a nice middle-class lady, the old-fashioned kind you used to see in women's magazines when I was a teenager, who take good care of themselves and know exactly what to do when their husbands stray; I had slipped into the role, even to the point of needing to ask him for money, like a kept woman, with the same comfortable feeling as slipping on an elegant fur coat. I was sitting down as I said it, and I just managed to avoid crossing my legs and putting my elbow on my thigh, cupping my chin in my hand. Many years before, after an extremely painful incident, another stereotype had fleetingly come to my aid, in a similar way. When my mother killed herself, all the other members of my close family, my maternal grandmother who had lived with us, my father and my brother, had died before her, so I had had to face the violence of her suicide without the support of their intimacy and understanding. For years I had remained convinced that this crisis had robbed me of the secure belief in my future which I had held since my childhood, but I couldn't actually make out the particular aims which I felt I had been obliged to give up, and all this gave me a sense of powerlessness which was disconcerting to the woman who had grown up from the little girl steeped in literature and bursting with ambition. I had tried to express all this to Jacques one day, and all I could come up with was the phrase: 'My mother's death has broken me.'

'What kind of cliché is that?' he answered, rather brusquely, though with the best of intentions, to help me find a way out of the crisis. Being caught *in flagrante* using a ready made formula only increased my feelings of helplessness and humiliation. But over the next few days I had decided that in fact I wouldn't retract the word 'broken', even if it was so often used incorrectly, hyperbolically, creating the reverse effect of what was originally intended, and making it sound somehow pompous. There is a reason why a commonplace is called common. When we use one, it is not just that we suddenly have a lapse of lucidity or intelligence or even of culture, which would otherwise enable us to make a more refined or appropriate choice of vocabulary, it is also that we need to feel part of something. When suffering from the shock which comes from joy or misfortune, human beings are not fitted for the solitude which extreme emotions often bring upon them, and so they try to share them, which usually means they must 'relativise them', that is to say, play them down. True, I had spoken like someone in a TV show, but had I been given the chance I would actually happily have gone before the cameras to reassure myself that it was quite normal, and easy, to say that your mother was a depressive who threw herself out of a window, and to allow my suffering to dissolve in the burble of silly debate. When I suggested the facelift, I was projecting myself into the recognized role of the woman who believes in surface solutions, and during the period of utter devastation I found it soothing to become part of the great mass of simple thoughts. In addition to this I had already started to elaborate my fantasies regarding Jacques' sex life, according to the stereotyped framework I have mentioned, so that by adopting wholeheartedly a stereotyped form of behaviour, I brought them into the realm of real life. In other words, the stereotype and reality became fused in the same continuum of life. The age of the woman who had been betrayed, like the older man's taste for very young women, and society's mockery of the cuckold, are all fixed features of the imaginary world of sex and sentiment, and at least they provided me with some markers, albeit mediocre ones, and gave me the illusion of inhabiting a reality in which my fantasies were briefly prolonged. The episode about the woman who wants to make herself look younger, whose lines I could say in a real dialogue with Jacques, was a logical sequel to one of the episodes in which, for example, I burst in on him in the marital home in the company of a young female friend, and which, as it happens, was merely a bad daydream. It goes without saying that none of these were arguments which would supply Jacques with the key to understanding what was really upsetting me; they even made him less inclined to feel sorry for me.

Sometimes our discussions lasted late into the night, as we lay on our backs, side by side, like two recumbent statues, our eyes staring into a darkness less deep than theirs, but, like them, close yet separated by the runnel of a fold in the sheet. While the salt of my tears lay heavy on my cheek, and all my words seemed to be stuck together in a black substance which made my mouth feel bloated, I would find myself waiting, not for a word, but for a gesture. I would say to him: 'Do something.'

I would have liked some compassion, the kind I feel myself when I see a certain look in the eyes, for example, of an old person too physically weak to be able to see the world beyond their doorstep, or children from whom certain keys to this world have been hidden, or animals with their noses to the ground, trying to find their bearings, all incapable of making sense of the suffering which is crushing them. Their very being becomes one with their suffering and from their blank stares as they look up at the men and women who are aware of and have caused their plight, we see that they are held in its grasp. I truly believe that I also felt this when I suffered but could not communicate other than with simple words, without dipping deep into personal feelings. Perhaps he would have understood better if, instead of using clichés and getting into a twist over the minor distortions imposed by my fantasies on the insignif-icant facts of everyday life, I had started by sharing these fantasies with him. This never occurred to me, because my unconscious would never, I imagine, have been prepared to run the risk of trusting Jacques with the secret of my masturbatory visions, visions of him making love to other women. There was an incompatibility between my demanding his closest attention, as I did at such times, and simultaneously bending his ear about how his indifference and his disdain for me excluded me from his sex life. I looked for relief to the very person whom I had made the agent of my intolerable and delicious torment. The black mud in my mouth spread like coagulating lava, and soon the only organ I had left with any feeling in it was my skin, which I hoped Jacques would call upon, by sliding his index finger across it.

Occasionally, without a word, he would take hold of the lifeless puppet by his side and, now sitting, positioned between her thighs, would raise her hips. I let him do as he wished, and did not speak either, letting go of my limbs and my tumbling flesh and eventually the misery in which I had been submerged a few moments before would augment the wave of pleasure which swept me away. After which we finally went to sleep.

But the crisis did not always end like this, and the silence which swiftly descended between us was frequently of a different kind, which still puzzles me to this day. I have never understood the way Jacques increasingly chose to cut off our discussions by refusing to speak, I could never see what it was, at any precise moment, that made him do this. He would turn over on his side, I would ask if he was angry, he would say no, and it was over, I got no further response, I might have another shot the next day, and again the day after that, buttress myself against his arm, call his name as though I had spotted him retreating into the distance, or else, by speaking very quietly, try to make him believe that the crisis was over, or ask him at least to tell me which word or reproach of mine had hurt him, but he would move away, assure me that we had to let time do its work, that it would blow over; and so it would, maybe two, three or four days later, though I still had no idea why he had changed his mind, he would speak to me about something completely ordinary and this time the tone and the flow of his voice would be casual. I may have found the mysterious figure of my daydreams attractive, but faced with the mysteries of the real person I was completely at a loss. During these periods of silence, Jacques' face was like that of someone you see making his way down the street, impassive, deep in his thoughts, who, if he bumps into someone by mistake, apologises politely, without meeting their eye. The worst thing was that Jacques' indifference towards me, as conjured up in my fantasies, threw me into panic when he showed it for real. I was incapable, then, of foreseeing, and then waiting for the moment when he would speak to me again – or rather, I was plunged for all eternity into this state of waiting.

So that, as time went by, I would feel proud if I could count eight or ten days during which, even if our relationship had been tense, we had not argued. I had not allowed myself to be sucked in by the vortex of the stairway leading to his office or, if I had, then I had stifled the demands for explanations which sooner or later ensued. It was around this time that I started to become interested in the statements of men who had committed rape, principally repeat offenders, whom I might have seen on the television, or whose comments I had read in articles, and who described the same process I had come to recognize on my own scale. They almost all spoke not of a madness which blinded them and stopped them seeing the consequences of their act, but, on the contrary, of a lucid feeling of strength, a powerful light shining on the drama in which they are the active agent. It is almost as though this lucidity had the same power of injunction as the spotlights trained on an actor when he comes onto the stage. Far from preventing any occurrence of the evil act, the knowledge one has of it surrounds it with a sparkle which makes it all the more attractive: you recognize the awakening of the drive, you are fully aware of the ravages it will cause, you are still capable of mobilizing your moral resources, your faculty of reasoning, in an attempt to repress it, but nothing can stop the act which, in the end, you commit. Only then does all turn black, the fog of remorse and guilt invades the mind, because the purpose of the drive was, it turns out, not just to blot out certain parts of one's conscience, but to sweep the whole thing aside; the drive only kept it alive the better to destroy it. When, having carefully chosen my words, then decided it was better to say nothing and to support my decision with a thousand arguments, including the possibility that Jacques would put up a wall of silence, which would be even worse than the doubt which was gnawing at me now, when, afflicted by a sudden amnesia which blocked out all this logic, I heard myself utter the fatal question, I was in fact creating the conditions of the destiny which I had reserved for myself in my dreams: rejected from Jacques' life, I was destroyed.

It was later that I realized there was a link between masturbation, voyeurism and the pleasures of restraint and exclusion. The masturbator is the spectator of his own fantasies, whether he takes them from pornographic pictures and writing, or creates them out of memories of scenes personally experienced or extrapolated on the basis of real events; that is to say, he responds principally to a visual stimulus. In certain circumstances, he may have the pleasure of a live performance; in such cases the masturbator becomes a voyeur. Now, the voyeur stalks his visions secretively, shut away, to a greater or lesser degree, in a hiding place; at least he restricts his movements and breathing to avoid discovery, or so as not to disturb the people who are coupling in front of him, if they are aware of his presence. In all cases, he mentally removes himself from the scene, even if he is its orchestrator, as Dalí was of those evening events where, he tells us, he instructed the others in their movements, but himself touched no one's sex but his own. The same Dalí who in the end admitted that he 'needed no one'. This habit of standing to one side, of hiding away, goes back a long way: the child who masturbates, under the twofold threat of punishment and shame, has no choice but to dissim-ulate and, as a result, if he is not prepared to give up the pleas-ure, and becomes someone who likes to watch copulation, as performed either in his dreams or by other people, will turn into a habitué of the world beneath the duvet, of closets, cup-boards and doorways, even perhaps of keyholes, where the eyes slide through while the body remains awkwardly crouched, as though the whole thing had to pass through, a habit for which, in accordance with the law which automati-cally links the circumstances of a thrill to the thrill itself, he may well acquire a taste. A masturbator likes solitude, or rather, tries to sustain the – by now delightful – sensation of being forced into solitude, that is to say, driven out of, expelled from the public arena. Salvador Dalí, that 'great masturbator' (to quote the title of one of his famous paintings) and great paranoiac (like that great dreamer, Jean-Jacques Rousseau), worked out a strange formal theory which accounts for this condition: he asserted that matter takes shape when, subjected to coercion by space itself, it blisters and overflows. He must have felt that he himself was 'formed' in this way, when he gave this account of his one and only experience of the metro: he had felt as though he was being 'squeezed by an intestine', but, at the moment at which he was 'vomited' and 'spat out' from it, he experienced the 'revelation' of a 'creative rebirth'(the theme of birth, and the possibility, for the artist, of reliving the expulsion from the mother's womb, or being reborn, recurs frequently in his work). Surely it is significant that the odd feeling I mentioned having while playing with my family – though without my mother – in the park at Saint-Cloud, when my turn was skipped because I had been forgotten and had become invisible even while remaining part of the group, is linked in my memory to the time when I first started my periods. Throughout much of my life, like many women, I have felt, during the days preceding the start of my period, that the people close to me had stopped loving me, and even while I found this upsetting, I would derive a sweet satisfaction from it. And I am quite prepared to believe that my determination at work, which is widely acknowledged, and my ability, when everyone around me is busy or having fun, to focus on a task for long periods at a time, occasionally punctuated by inter-ludes of onanism, are both attempts to discover a similar sort of pleasure. Work, including work which is freely chosen, is the means by which society exerts pressure on the individual. But when someone finds their work utterly absorbing, it also becomes their escape route. And there is also an analogy between the way the psyche submits to constraints in order to find delicious ways of getting free of them, and the way the penis or clitoris, under pressure or friction from the masturba-tor's hand, eventually explodes and escapes into orgasm.

. . . . .

The little passage you go through to get to our flat has a low ceiling and is usually unlit, a sort of vestibule, where the space briefly closes in, between the series of courtyards behind you and the first room, which is surprisingly large. It is scarcely more than a metre wide, just enough for me to throw my body from one wall to the other in a single movement. I hit the wall not just with my head or the palms of my hands, my whole upper body or shoulders smacked against it too. It was a violent but slow movement, concentrated and rhythmic. Jacques stopped it by placing his arms around me.

When I think about these outbursts, I realize how precious are the little fragments of images from pictures, from books or paintings, from photographs, or spectacles of any kind, which gather in the depths of our memory and end up cementing the emotional inheritance which is unique to each of us. This is where we find the models with which we can compare the circumstances of our own lives, and the way we choose to react to them, they form a base on which we can stand the questions which torment us. If our personality makes us sensitive to a certain work, or to certain details in this work, it may be that the work itself, or the detail, will dictate to us, by a perfect dialectic, a particular attitude or action. And just as a painter who sets up his easel in the middle of nature does not actually paint nature, but sees it through the filter of his references to other painters, what we call our 'nature', our spontaneous demonstrations of love, hate, joy and despair, bears the stamp of our reading and our aesthetic preferences. Years before, when I was writing about the painting of Jackson Pollock, one aspect of it in particular had attracted my attention: when he rolled out his canvas on the floor, he was deliberately seeking out the resistance of a hard surface, in contrast with the suppleness of the canvas stretched over a frame. I had been struck, when I saw Hans Namuth's film about Pollock, by the way the artist made his drip paintings by moving sideways along the edge, placing his foot flat on the ground, as though he was tapping a rhythm. And I have always seen the zipper in the pictures of Barnett Newman as a bleeding incision in a vast, hermetic surface. The singular theme of the body meeting a hard or sealed surface must be a particular concern with me (and this goes back to well before my mother's suicide, judging by its correspondence with my work on Pollock and Newman), because I came across it again when I was writing about Yves Klein, notably about his Anthropometries, and again, years after the episode I have been describing, this time in connection with Dalí. On the basis of these examples I conclude that anyone who feels their eyes irresistibly drawn towards a seamless flow or spread of colour, or towards the infinite blue of the sky, or the sequence of hallucinations characteristic of the paranoid-critical method, will also feel the need to hold fast to their body. Thus, in the work of Yves Klein, we find both the longing for the infinite represented in the blue monochromes, the appropriation of empty space, and the impact of the body against an impassable surface. I automatically picked out in Dalí's writings all the allusions to contact with this kind of surface, as when he notes in *The Secret Life of Salvador Dalí* that he slept on a bed which was so hard that it 'seemed to be stuffed with dry bread', but which 'had the virtue' of reminding him that he did actually have a body.

This inheritance does not really allow us to analyse the crazed and sometimes monstrous behaviour of which we are capable,

or which we meet in others, but it does help us to accept it –
without going completely mad – by relating it to models drawn
from a noble and often more abstract register and which, in the
heat of the moment, may offer some kind of explanation. One
function of art is to lift us up out of our condition, but
another – and this is irrespective of how good it is, or how
sophisticated – is to supply each of us, according to our cultural background, with talismans to help us find our bearings
in the everyday world, and in the ebb and flow of our feelings.

'You're completely mad,' Jacques would tell me, without of
course meaning it in its strongest sense, but rather as you
would say 'he's mad', 'she's mad', about someone whose
behaviour is extreme, or excessive, or rash, and he said it
simply because it drove him mad to see me in this state. But I
must in fact have partly lost my mind for the physical pain I
felt at hitting the wall to have had the effect of relieving some
of the emotional pain. Later, the memory came back to haunt
me, mortify me, but I found myself able to superimpose the
image of Pollock working, or of the women who were Klein's
models with their air of indifference and simple concentration
as they pressed as much of the surface of their flesh as they
could against a large sheet of paper fixed to the wall, none of
these examples actually unlocked the mystery of my behaviour,
but they provided the outline of a sort of paradigm into which
it might fit, which allowed me to admit to it, rather than
simply throw it down to the bottom of the bottomless pit of
repressed thoughts. This is the minimum of rational thought
of which we are capable. Similarly, a researcher who discovers
an unknown object puts it away in a drawer or assigns it a

category on the basis of a simple formal analogy, until such time as he can verify the accuracy of his classification.

What fleeting images do we get of our own bodies during the course of our everyday lives? What visual fragments flash across the mind when, for example, we meet someone: that of our hand taking hold of theirs in greeting, or the purely mental image of the face we present to them? If we were on the look-out for it, would the conjunction of the two reveal a monster with a head but no body, with a single arm protruding from a vague area somewhere below the chin? And what about when we make love? If I offer the man my back, as I like to, the image I have in my mind is mostly of my backside, an image I myself find arousing, as though I were merging with Jacques' point of view. I have noticed that when I am lying on my back, my mental field of vision is invaded by an image of my vagina, an immense cavern lit with a chiaroscuro effect. I don't see the tensing of my face, which Jacques perhaps briefly glimpses, but I sometimes imagine it when I am masturbating on my own. The truth is, we tend not to dwell on these images, because as long as we are healthy in body and calm of spirit, our instinctive perception of them is amazingly plastic. But what happens to this intuition when our consciousness is slowed down or clouded by emotion and the sole means of expression becomes the body? As far as I can recall, when I reached the point at which I could no longer express anything which anyone would understand, I also felt that all I could see was a disparate jumble of limbs. The light, fluid sense of entirely occupying one's body was transformed into a pure reflex of resistance to two opposing and equally powerful forces. There was the molten flow of words which could not be uttered because there was no point, which paralysed my tongue as far back as the glottis, and made my body rigid, and there was everything outside of me, the walls of the room, the ceiling, Jacques' back, as he lay facing away from me, all of which formed a single block, which pushed me away. Is it possible to inhabit a body which has no space, within or without, to call its own? When a crisis arose during the course of one of our discussions in bed, one leg, always the same one, the right leg, would start to vibrate like a string which has been tightened. As I have said, I had perhaps already tried to call out to the one whom I made both my judge and my court of appeal. 'Jacques! Jacques!' I said, over and over: 'Jacques! Jacques!', or sometimes: 'Oh please… please!' The crises came quite often (I'm trying to work it out now: perhaps one or two a month?) and I learned to see them coming, though I could not hold them back, no more than I could the question which had sparked off the discussion. The hands were the only parts that moved, revolving round the wrists, and the fingers, which stretched and then folded again, but all independently, in a slowed down, stuttering deaf-mute language; perhaps it was an attempt to unpick the knot of tangled words. Finally, the palm of one hand mechanically hit the mattress, in the conventional gesture of a wrestler who is pinned to the ground and submits to his opponent. Or I would watch these same hands waving about, against the sloping ceiling, fingers stretched wide. I tried to stave off the feeling that I was suffocating, which, once again, I can only connect to a memory of something I have read: the terror which had haunted me for years, after reading Edgar Allen Poe as a child, that one day I might be buried alive. Then the fists closed tight and Jacques could not prise them open.

I swung up into a sitting position, as though coming up from a somersault, and the fists came up to beat at the skull, the face, the chest. As when I had thrown myself against the wall, the physical pain was strong enough to absorb me, and the precise moment at which it was keenest and most localized, unlocked the other pain, the all-consuming one that blots out everything else, including whatever caused it. The mechanism was rather similar to one which a physiotherapist once explained to me: he had advised me to press as hard as I could on the most painful point of a muscular spasm because there exists a sort of place beyond pain, such that when pain reaches its peak the brain puts up a fight and refuses to register it, affording a brief moment of respite.

At this point in my story I am rather short of images with which to describe those paroxysmal moments, I have run out of marker images, things once seen or 'read', which might help me to reconstruct them. I should now invite Jacques to take up the tale, but then the story would not issue, as it has from the very start, from inside a single body. The clearest impression I can recall is that of an enormous strength rising up inside me when Jacques tried to pin down my arms, hold my shoulders, a surprising feeling that my physical strength was going to dominate his, that I was filled with a kind of violence which was invincible. I weighed up whether I would be able to resist him, or fight him off, knowing it would have taken only a very slight extra effort, of which I was still capable, to hurl him to the ground. As this surpassing strength erupted, I would sometimes think how easy it would be to make a clean sweep, to destroy everything which only seconds earlier had been bearing down on top of me. It was this feeling, and not Jacques' gesture, which had only been a trigger, which took hold of me and revived a flicker of consciousness. After all, I'm not mad, and a third consideration began to emerge, ready to fight off the others, my own grasp of the situation, not, of course, a full understanding of how I had come to be in it, the reasons for my suffering or Jacques' reactions, no, it was rather a more prosaic sort of discernment, aimed at preventing me from harming Jacques, or breaking objects.

The first sign of reason is not reasoning but its apparent opposite, the automatic reflexes through which someone who has suffered a terrible misfortune, a bereavement, a serious illness, rather than soothing the pain or anguish with meta-physical reflection, organises the way his body moves among the objects around him, methodically considering the place of each one – setting about the housework, for example – or learns or relearns to nourish his body, as though he needed to retrace the entire course of human consciousness, starting with the basic steps for survival.

I am familiar with the physical pleasure of a good weep; at certain times in my life I would find myself sobbing as a pro-longation of orgasm. After my convulsions, the heaving of my chest acted like a valve for evacuating the pressure which had paralysed my limbs. They were not tears of rage, they were tears of remission, of despair, the tears we shed as children when we give up trying to have any influence on the world of adults and must simply leave it to them, abdicate our respon-sibility, like an animal or a slave. Sometimes, with their vague representations of suicide, my fantasies contributed to this relief. I do not think I have ever been seriously tempted by suicide, I don't believe I have the psychological make-up for it, but in this case, the idea allowed me to withdraw from a body which was in the grip of mental suffering. They were scarcely formed images, like scenes viewed through frosted glass, with no identifiable details, and sometimes, to ward off the false image, I would point two fingers and place them on my temple, or in my mouth.

While these crises were going on, I came to realize the extent to which my anticipation of satisfaction was centred on my mouth. I knew already that a moment of prolonged thought, or worry, instinctively made me put the index finger of my right hand, and even sometimes my thumb, in my mouth, because one day in the metro, when I was deep in my own thoughts and had slipped into this gesture in public, a stranger came up to me and teased me, saying: 'Ooh, that's not nice! At your age!' And of course I had always very much enjoyed oral sex. Sometimes, in that intermediary state in which we no longer know whether we are completely empty or too full to move, I would finally calm down, clinging to Jacques, my half-open lips pressed to the fleshy part of his arm, leaving a tiny suction imprint on it. Just then, the interior camera, which God gave me when he left, began to roll again, tirelessly resuming its surveillance. It showed me the full absurdity of my coiled-up body, too big, too mature for such infantile behaviour, but Jacques let me get on with it, and it didn't last very long, anyway, because I soon stopped, just letting my lips rest in the wet little pool of saliva they had deposited on his skin.

the blue room

The most violent crises occurred in the house in the Midi. I was less distracted by my social life than in Paris and could give myself over completely to my vision of Jacques indulging in a variety of priapic adventures. Both of us had the time to get involved in long discussions. The house itself exerted a far greater pressure on my paranoia. In theory, this house is much more the locus of our intimate life; and I was, accordingly, all the more aware of the presence of outside interference. Jacques spends more time there than I do; he had been there with various women friends. Despite the fact that the furniture and the objects we have there were chosen and arranged by both of us, I began to act like a visitor who moves about carefully and cautiously so as not to disturb an arrangement which is not her own. I was the three-dimensional version of an outline taken from an unknown source.

But that particular morning had been quiet. As was his habit, Jacques had gone out to buy the newspapers. I needed an envelope. I found one in a bundle on a shelf near his desk. It was the size I was looking for. When I opened it, I noticed it contained a piece of paper. Obviously, I should never have taken out the piece of paper, as Jacques repeatedly pointed out afterwards, but as we have seen, it had become an automatic reflex. I was drawn to it because I recognized, almost subliminally, a page from one of his notebooks. The first line said: 'I'm tearing out this page from my diary because I know Catherine reads it. This must not fall into her hands.'

I read that he is at *Le Pradié*, the house where our friend Bernard lives, in the Aveyron. Blandine has gone with him, and another friend of hers. He jokes about the way the two of them, mature men, are titillated by the presence of the two young women. They take photos of them, the girls undress at their request. Blandine shares his bed but refuses to have sex. Even so, he is able to caress her at length, and she falls asleep wrapped around him. There is a remark to the effect that she generally seems to have a low libido, and another about the shape of her breasts, or perhaps about how soft her skin is there. After a few days the friend has to go back to Paris, and they take her to the station. The date at the top of the page is a few weeks earlier.

I began to tremble so much that I had great difficulty holding the pen with which I immediately wrote to Jacques. When the mind begins to disintegrate, and our eyes land on objects right in front of us, but cannot transfix or interpret them, which is to say that the inner eye is unable to take over, then our limbs seem to collapse. As though we need to have ideas for our bodies to hold up! I didn't say much in my note. Simply that I had found the page, and otherwise I must have scribbled more or less the same words as the ones with which I attempted to ward off the crises: 'Jacques… please… It hurts too much… Help me… ' As my legs had gone from under me, I went and lay down on the bed.

I had not trembled like this, all over, since the day I received a call from the police station asking me to 'come as quickly as possible' because my mother had had 'an accident'. At my insistence, the voice eventually informed me that she had died. My legs were wobbly, but although my mind was partly numbed – a sudden death transports us at a stroke into a new life we know nothing about – my perception was still extremely sharp and focused: before I did anything else, I managed to walk as far as the bathroom and there I looked at myself in the mirror above the basin. I must have said out loud, for the benefit of my reflection 'My mother is dead' and heard my own voice ring out. I watched the effect this produced on the face looking back at me: eyes staring stupidly, features drawn, distorted – and I could actually feel the nerves tugging – tingling beneath the skin – the jaw shaking. The hypnotic power exerted by this image for a few seconds, which became etched in my memory, worked like pain relief. I had stopped suffering. Still staring at my own frightening reflection, I thought for a moment. Jacques was at the school where he taught, I would call Myriam, she had a car, she could drive me, and we would be there before midday. Every now and then I said to myself: 'She took some pills.' The reflection in the glass vanished, and I imagined my mother as I had seen her during the last few days, sitting on the edge of her bed, deathly pale, tufts of hair sticking out comically from her head, from having lain so long against the pillow, her thin nightdress pulled up around her thighs. She was putting pills in her mouth and greedily slugging back a glass of water. When I think about her death now, that is one of the two images which come to mind, the other being the one I really saw, of the still open window out of which she had thrown herself and, outlined against the light, the stool she had placed in front of it.

I had left the note for Jacques, with his page beside it, in an obvious place on the kitchen table. I now have no idea what I was thinking about as I went and lay down in my usual place, on my back, my body straight, my eyes open but unseeing. There can have been no room left for interpretation or speculation, just vacant anticipation of Jacques' return. I saw him open the bedroom door, but he seemed to be at a great distance. It is a large bedroom, but the distance from where I was on the bed to the door was exaggerated, as in an expressionist drawing where the vanishing point is placed high up, to accentuate the perspective. I heard him saying over and over: 'What have I done? Oh, what have I done...' He held the torn out page in his hand. He came up close. His face was as indistinct as that of someone in a dream. In fact, I was witnessing the scene from the same indeterminate place one occupies in a dream, where one is omniscient but at the same time unable to communicate. More than anything, I heard him. He was saying he should never have done it, he knew perfectly well, 'Look, watch...' ; I realized he was tearing up the page. He must have crouched down to take hold of my hands or arms, but I was too far away to feel his touch. I had no sense even of my own presence. It was as though he was acting out the scene alone, with, before him, a pool of acid, which was gradually devouring the real world. I asked him 'Will Jacques come?... Will somebody come?'

He may have wept, but I'm not very sure. I must have been caught in a kind of time warp. Jacques' words, his entire demeanor, were everything I had wished for each time I had imagined that in the end, if I explained just once more, he would understand me. He didn't turn my questions back at me, he didn't get angry. He said how sorry he was, he was affectionate, he leaned over me like a father over his sick child. We all have in our hearts a deep nostalgia for our childhood illnesses, during which we lay huddled in the damp sheets, dimly aware of the anxious voices of those around us, carefully lowered, and muffled by the fever. But the scene I had waited for for so long remained unreal. For so long I had been settled in this state of waiting, which cut me off from the world, that I couldn't come out of it. The prisoner who had so longed for her freedom, and who had developed the habit of projecting herself into a hypothetical future, could not now believe in the existence of the warder who, just at the moment when a terrible sentence had been passed, was opening the door; by reflex she hid away at the back of her cell.

In another scene which came after this one – but I couldn't say whether it was the same day or the next – I am still in the bedroom, this time standing next to Jacques. I put my arm round him and it feels as though I am much taller than him. I speak gently and I tell him that we will take care of little Blandine, that she needs us, that we'll take good care of her. I'm feeling better. I have emerged from my isolation and my words come easily. My determination that Jacques should come to my aid and the sense that he can't hear me have gone. Now I am the one who takes his head in my hands and strokes it. He speaks quietly, with a slight catch in his voice, saying over and over: 'Stop, stop…'

If someone has a fall and clings to a branch by a huge effort, is there a split second in which he feels an absurd sense of relief, as his strength gives out and he releases his grip and allows himself to fall into the void? I had let go, and during the short time it took to glide down, felt a moment of reprieve. Something would happen: Jacques, or someone else, would make an allusion which suddenly illuminated some corner of his mystery life. Fearing the agony of a complete discovery, I would close my eyes to it. For example, Jacques had taken me to see a film. I was just about to tell a friend when she interrupted me, saying: 'Oh, Jacques and I went to the cinema too the other day!' And she would supply the title which was just on the tip of my tongue. At this I began to let myself slide. It never lasted very long, it was rather like the jolt you feel when your heel slips on the last step and you regain your balance. I fled from the little patch of hell in which I would have had to ask myself why Jacques had gone back with me to see a film which he had seen the day before, or two days earlier, with one of our friends. I said the first thing I thought of, the first ready-made, anodyne phrase which came to mind; it was usually more or less, though not always, appropriate to the situation: 'It was very full…' or, 'It'll be ok…', and I would repeat it mechanically. I would have found conversation too painful, and it swiftly came to an end. I became a sort of extra, with no attributes, my words had no impact, I was present but did not exist.

Long after this episode, I read in Simone de Beauvoir's *Memoirs* 'the story of Louise Perron', a story which threw light on certain bizarre psychological mechanisms. I will not compare my own case to that of this woman, which de Beauvoir terms a 'tragedy'! Louise Perron was a thirty-year-old virgin, who was seduced and abandoned. To avoid accepting reality, she had developed a delirium which was serious enough for her to end up in a clinic. But she was an intelligent woman, and de Beauvoir reports that she was able to refer to her own behaviour as a 'charade', saying she was going to stop 'monkeying about', but that the moment she hit upon a reasonably realistic means of escape from it, she would burst out laughing, saying that 'that too was a charade!' She had confessed to de Beauvoir that she had experienced a kind of 'splitting of her personality', adding 'how horrible it was, constantly to see oneself'. It is clear that there are some psychic states in which the person comes to produce at least two avatars of himself, each one with its own consciousness, which makes it possible to judge the other, but with no third, as it were, intermediary consciousness to take a final decision as to which is better, or less bad, than the other.

Most of the time I was reacting, if I am to describe it from the point of view I had then, to a real danger. Take, for example, the time when we were having a rather pleasant dinner, just the two of us, in a restaurant we liked very much in Venice, where we were the last remaining customers. At the end of the meal I had the feeling that when he described the way I looked in a certain outfit, Jacques was actually talking about another woman. I felt tears coming to my eyes, and to avoid bursting into sobs in front of the waitress who was watching us, and more than anything to ward off the anger I could sense welling up in him, I uttered four or five incoherent words. In a fraction of a second, the register changed. Where there had been an incipient domestic tiff, there was now the beginning of some kind of insignificant conversation. By reflex I had pressed the remote control and it was as though suddenly, a voice pitched at too high a volume, the voice-over to an advert, for example, suddenly silenced the snivelling heroine of a weepy old movie. I became aware of being out of sync even as I was speaking. I could hear myself: my tone was insistent, higher than normal, and seemed to fill my whole head. At the same time, I went on speaking nonsense for several moments, weakly allowing myself to be carried along by my own words until the impending crisis moved off. It didn't always stop it coming, but it did reduce it. Jacques allowed himself not to comment. He too was waiting for it to pass.

On the other hand, the time I realized that Jacques had seen the same film twice running, my thought was not that he had a special relationship with this friend. Not that such a relationship would have been implausible, our friend wasn't ugly, or a shrew. But I knew her too well, she was too close to me, and as a result she did not have the aura which would have destined her for the secret world in which Jacques was operating. Nor could I envisage that Jacques had quite simply gone with this friend to the cinema one day when I was away, that he had liked the film and wanted me to see it too, but had concealed from me the fact that he had already seen it, knowing it would make me suspicious. He had not foreseen that his little secret would put me on the scent of a much bigger mystery, more impenetrable than a liaison with this friend – and more fascinating!

We often went to stay at *Le Pradié*. It is like a house in a child's drawing: a front door and steps in the middle of the façade, two perfectly symmetrical windows on each side, a row of windows above, and a steeply sloping roof. The life we led there suited me well. We all got on with our own things: Bernard painted in the atelier, which was separated from the house by a huge, bowl-shaped lawn; his wife, Martine, who spent much of her time in Paris, working, was busy round the house, fixing things; Jacques read, in the garden in the summer, and in winter by the large fireplace in the kitchen; I myself worked in the bedroom known as the 'purple room', the one we were usually given, at a table which Martine had covered with an Indian shawl. The nib of my pen sank into it if I was not careful to put several thicknesses of paper underneath the page I was writing on.

The bedroom is situated above the kitchen. At the end of the day, when Bernard, then Martine had come to join Jacques, their conversations, with Bernard's emphatic inflections, Jacques' lower, steadier pitch, Martine's hoarse tones, along with their shouts of laughter, came up quite clearly through the floorboards. Sometimes they would decide to watch the news, and their voices mingled with the muffled accompaniment of the television. Then I would hear the percussion of the kitchen pots and pans. It was as marvellous as the world discovered by the princess at whose feet the earth opens to reveal the teeming kitchen which Riquet de la Houppe has had set up in preparation for their wedding. They called me when the meal was ready. It was understood that I did not participate in the preparation of meals. I had the status of a schoolgirl who must not be disturbed during study hours. But I was not disturbed by the noises below. Quite the opposite, they made me all the more aware that being imprisoned in one's work is a sweet constraint. Once I was ill and had to stay in bed for several days. My ears missed nothing of the joyful and generous life below me, and again I derived a kind of cosy pleasure from being excluded. I had been so happy there, within the shadowy walls of the purple room, so replete with my work, my solitude and, intermittently, the hubbub of the people I loved, that mentally, nostalgically, I still occupied it and therefore could not imagine putting Jacques and Blandine in bed together there.

Next to the purple room there is another, larger, lighter

room, the 'blue room'. I don't know why, but we had almost never stayed in this room. Once the episode of the torn out page had sunk in, the few brief phrases Jacques had used to describe his nights with Blandine formed the basis of what became one of my most recurrent visions during masturbation. The blue room, then, became the setting. I pictured them here, lying in the bed, the head of which is in an alcove. So, having denied Blandine the purple room, I was nevertheless giving her my place in the bed in the blue room! All communal life, starting with that shared by only two individuals, has the annoying tendency to assign each member a regular place: each person sits at the same chair each meal time, lies on the same side of the bed at home and in hotels. In real life, I never slip into an unknown bed without balking inwardly at these habits, which are adopted unthinkingly and rarely questioned. Within the walls whose limits we already accept, such habits oblige us, moreover, to tread in our own footsteps, sit where we've always sat, place our bodies each time in exactly the same spot in relation to other people's bodies. We like to think that we move about freely, but most of the time all we are doing is slipping into invisible tunnels which our bodies, like blind termites, have dug for us. Despite my irritation with these minideterminisms, they are so strong that even in my fantasy life I could not stop myself putting Jacques in his place in the bed and thus Blandine in mine. Also, Blandine lay in a position I often adopt myself: lying on her left side, slightly curled up. Jacques pressed up against her back and buttocks, in a position he also likes to adopt with me, which I like too, and often ask him for.

Contrary to what you might expect in such a scene, the room was crudely lit by a too-yellow light hanging from the ceiling, which is just as the lighting was in real life, and I had never liked it. Clearly it was only my inner eye I was seeking to please. Blandine might have taken my place, but I was not taking hers. I remained an observer. My imagined scenario followed the playing out of her reticence. She allowed herself to be caressed for a long, long time, she let Jacques part her buttocks, she might furtively, gently return his caresses. In one version, she even stood naked in the middle of the room and wriggled provocatively before joining him between the sheets. Jacques was bringing himself off: I kept close track of his mounting exasperation. He climaxed alone, his sex gripped tight in his hand, his body completely doubled up in a succession of little shudders. Sometimes I imagined Blandine passing through Bernard's room, where she acted out the same little scene. I don't now know whether Jacques came to join them or whether he stayed away, just to add to the frustration. Among the masturbatory fantasies which I used before what I might well call the period in which they were banished, and to which I have since returned, there is one in which I am fastened naked to a sort of wooden stake, in the middle of a group, principally of men, also naked, and a few women mingling with them, who are present but have no form (in accordance with the mind's ability to bring into existence beings who, even in a concrete context, remain ideas, moving through it like currents of air). These people are coupling before my eyes, they brush against me as they pass, but I must wait a long time, and loudly call for someone to come and attend to me, spread my legs wide, wiggle my hips and thrust my pubis forward as far as my bindings permit, becoming aroused almost to the point of exasperation, before someone finally agrees to unleash me and penetrate me. At which moment I release my spasm of pleasure.

in the door frame

Many years earlier I had been in analysis. Although I had always believed it had been beneficial, and those who knew me, finding me less withdrawn, less aggressive, confirmed this, to the point where one friend jokingly said that the psychoanalysts should have paid me (reimbursed me!) for being such a good advertisement for them, I have only a vague recollection of many aspects of it. I find it hard to recall exactly why I felt I should embark on it, and what made me decide, after four years, to stop, and even more so to remember what was said during the sessions, apart from a few anecdotes which later made good stories to swap with other ex-analysands, like those that circulate between former pupils of a school, for whom it is a way of letting off aggression towards the authority which formerly ruled over them.

My parents were still alive, and perhaps my relationship with them, particularly with my mother, who experienced periodic bouts of serious depression, kept me embroiled in the difficulties of childhood and adolescence, even though I am inclined to think now that my brutal uprooting from the family circle (I ran away from home, then came back, then left again for good) had perhaps made it necessary for me to exaggerate these difficulties so that I could justify my flight to myself and others. To be sure, I had grown up in an atmosphere of constant arguments, punctuated by shouts and blows, between my father and mother, between my mother and her mother, and my brother and myself; I had come to suspect quite early on that my father's absences, and the regular presence of a male friend of my mother's in our house, did not add up to the picture of a straightforward family. But other, happier memories were mixed in with the painful ones (my mother, whom I considered pretty, and who taught me to flirt; my complicity with my father, whose life seemed all the more attractive to me for being lived at arm's length from the rest of the family; the holidays in Quiberon, in a house at the end of a long, narrow garden, separated from a huge sports field by a wall which we could easily climb over, a house so tiny it reminded one of those little houses made of cloth or cardboard where children pretend to hide...). I had dealt with all these ups and downs with a certain bluster: it conferred a kind of uniqueness on me, which I liked to boast about, a knowingness about life which I vaunted in the playground. Until the time, some years later, when, like many very young adults, particularly those familiar with some of the rudiments of psychoanalysis, I felt the need to affirm my identity by making up stories and, in the process, dramatizing the early period of my life. I had endless conversations with a male friend my own age, the son of a very young and flighty mother, and a father he had never known. We nicknamed ourselves 'David Copperfield'. It was meant as a joke, but we believed it, a bit.

I went through analysis during the last few years of living with Claude, during which time, caught up in the muddle of emotions which result from sexual impatience, we had more and more rows, to the point where I had the depressing sense that I was reliving with him the kind of relationship my parents had had. I was beginning to grow closer to Jacques, which also highlighted the degree to which my life with Claude was out of sync. It was also complicated by our disagreements about how *Art Press* should be run. Since we had left the hushed streets of Bois-Colombes, I had unswervingly supported his every move, but when the magazine we had founded together began to run into financial difficulty and we had to take decisions about its future, I opposed him. Claude was authoritarian, and I, in a less obvious way, was just as determined, and I experienced the whole work situation as an inner conflict.

When people asked me, I would say that it was when my only brother, who was three years younger than me, was killed in an accident that I decided to enter analysis. It was a clear-cut, plausible answer, which spared me from having to expand further. But in fact this event must have been decisive, not because I found I needed help to get over the pain but, on the contrary, because it unleashed a new vitality in me, by way of reaction. I have suffered greatly from this loss, and as long as I live I will regret not being able to continue to share my child-hood, under the outer packaging of adulthood, with my brother. But after the first few weeks, during which I felt the inevitable guilt of the person left living when someone else dies prematurely and unfairly, and having consciously put my misery to the test by asking myself pertinent questions, such as whether I would have preferred to lose an arm or my eye-sight than him, I felt the weight of a new responsibility, a huge desire to act, almost as though I were on drugs. I was the daughter, but I had inherited the family name, the sole anchor point in the familial swamp. I had lots of plans for *Art Press*. I was well aware that neurotic upheavals would get in the way. The person I called, asking him to make some enquiries and recommend me a psychoanalyst, was Jacques.

Three times a week I got out of the metro at Saint-Michel and walked halfway back up the boulevard, then up the rue Soufflot, at the top of which was the consulting room of Dr C. M., carrying my little bag full of ruminations which, as I say, I would find it hard, now, to recall. The unravelling of the tangle of family life? The behaviour of my mother, by which I felt harassed? Being torn between Claude and Jacques? Whatever it was, the sessions must have had a liberating effect on my mind because as I hurried my way back down the boulevard, along which are a large number of cheap clothes shops, I always had my neck twisted round so as not to miss anything of the window displays, and I still remember the delight I took in my few, modest purchases! One of the very few subjects we discussed during my sessions on the couch, which now comes back to me spontaneously, is linked to my reading of Virginia Woolf's novel, *Orlando*. Even then, it is tied to the fact that the analyst asked me to bring him the book, then made me wait several days when I asked him some time later to return it, and ended up by telling me he had lost it, which added to the unease I had felt while reading the book. As a result, I have never reread it, since I never bought it again. Could it be that the character of Orlando, who changes sex during the course of the story, touched me because I had just lost my own male double?

But more than the various woes of childhood, more than the difficulties of living with another person, the main cause of my unhappiness was probably an ambition hidden away deep inside me, a hardy shoot which had sustained me in childhood, and around which had twined the ivy of my dreams, but which, in the belief that I was now realizing them, I had stifled? At twelve, naïve and conformist, I was convinced, though I would never have dared say so, that I wanted to write, either poems or novels. At eighteen, I simply wanted to write. At twenty-two I had been publishing articles in art magazines for two years. I had quickly carved out a respected niche in the professional milieu I had been aiming for. At twenty-four I started my own magazine. And yet the busier I got at work, the deeper my ambition sank into the shifting sands of my unconscious and there, forgotten, it remained, dissatisfied, though I could not put my finger on the causes of this dissatisfaction. Everything I had achieved had been so in line with the smooth logic of my early dreams that I had never really outgrown their comforting promises, and never understood that it was not enough to have desires, that sometimes you had to make a determined effort to achieve them, to force the hand of fate. Since school and parents had ceased to be the ones to dictate what I did, and how I behaved, I had gone with the flow of chance encounters, opportunities I had grasped but never created myself. Claude certainly showed more determination in the setting up of the magazine than I did. All the same, since I took it over, my commitment has always been total, whatever the difficulties.

To sum up, I had the will and the determination, but no objective. I firmly believe that the desire to write presents itself as a necessity, and that the verb 'to write', like the verb 'to breathe', occurs initially in the intransitive form. As long as the word applied to articles and essays on art, I could convince myself I was responding to this necessity, but without realizing that I was waiting for the good fairy, the fortuitous encounter with a master or older person, who, in accordance with the myth (*cf*. Kris and Kurz!) would push me to write differently, about something else, and this expectation created a void inside me, on the brink of which I sometimes experienced a vague sense of anxiety.

I thought about going back into analysis; I mentioned it to Jacques, and we discussed it across the same table near which I had told him I had discovered the photographs of the pregnant girl with no clothes on, but this time I had my elbows on the table and was looking directly at him. More than a year had passed, the crises were exhausting both of us and isolating us in our own closed world. I don't think Jacques had confided in anyone – Bertrand, maybe, but he did not see him very often – and the only times I myself would have appreciated a third person, an intercessor whom I could have asked to translate the things I could not explain myself, was during the actual moments of crisis: on occasions I found myself repeating mechanically, once I had calmed down a bit, that I 'needed someone', but the someone I wanted was probably just an omniscient and all-merciful Jacques. I would not have known who else to turn to. It is possible that my circle of acquaintances picked up on signs of my disturbance, that one of my friends might have noticed an unusual sadness, that a neighbour might have heard me weeping, that when we were out walking my companions perhaps found my remarks a little strange. Sometimes I thought I detected surprise on their part, and then I tried to take a grip of myself, not because I wished to protect myself, but to avoid having to explain. A couple of experiences early on in life taught me that if there was one thing I hated it was confidences, both receiving other people's and giving my own, and in my view true shamelessness lay there, not in the act of making one's private life public through writing or pictures. Confidences oblige the person being spoken to to reciprocate – the speaker is looking for attention, advice, compassion from the listener, who must acknowledge his responsibility, whereas there is always a distance between the public and a person who puts themselves on display, even if the distance is the height of the stage for the performance of a stripper, who expects nothing more from her anonymous audience than the conventional reaction of applause.

When I thought about psychoanalysis, it was with a sort of detachment, as though I knew nothing about it and was responding resignedly to a sound piece of advice, and it was one of those decisions which, once taken, you quickly start to talk about, because the spoken word consolidates it and stops you turning back. Then there was the problem of money. I earned next to nothing at *Art Press*. We agreed that Jacques would advance me the money and I would pay him back gradually, with the extra I earned from prefaces to catalogues, lectures, and trying to cut back where I could. The next morning, when I got to work, I immediately asked the receptionist to look up the address and telephone number of Dr M. She would find it for me straight away; she was an intelligent, cheerful girl, whom I liked very much. I was amazed at my own cheeriness, the ease with which the whole process was getting underway, even though I knew how long and difficult it would be. I made the call. The good thing with psychoanalysts is you get to speak to them in person: there is no intimidating secretary with a bossy voice offering you an appointment two months hence; they speak very close to the receiver, a soft voice draws you in, immediately you are in their presence. Even so, I had taken a moment to practise what I would say before picking up the phone: 'I am Catherine Millet, I was one of your analysands years ago and I would like to come and see you again.'

Since I had stopped my visits to rue Soufflot, I had had to deal with my father's and then, a few months later, my mother's – violent – death. For a long time I had to organize my life around the need for constant vigilance, the result of her mental condition, around her daily early morning phone calls, which often roused me from my sleep, the visits, to her home or the hospital, during which I tried without success to drag the drowning body, heavier than my own, up into the open air, and the meetings with the doctors who were caring for her, whose opinions were as contradictory as her own behaviour. She would draw me towards her to kiss her, then immediately yell because, as I leaned over towards her, I had nudged the drip by which she was being fed and had hurt her. This was, too, a decisive period for the future of the magazine, which also worried me, but in a different way. Even so, it had never remotely occurred to me that I might go back into analysis, even when the only thing left I could think of to say was 'My mother's death has broken me'. I summarised all this for Dr M., and finished by saying that the last straw was that I, who had always been the paragon of sexual freedom, should find myself back with him on account of something not unlike a bedroom farce. He replied by lifting two fingers from the armrest of his chair. My last session with him had been twenty years ago. At the beginning of our conversation he told me I 'hadn't changed'. At the time I took it as a polite remark which affected me rather in the same way as the business of the cosmetic surgery, or when I had that discussion with the taxi driver: a sort of assurance of normality. I think I was sitting up rather straight in my chair, and it felt a bit as if we were chatting at some social event. Then, as soon as I was back outside, I decided he must surely have been making an allusion to the fact that, in all this time, I hadn't made much progress in resolving my inner conflicts. I was off.

When I think about this second series of sessions, which, each time, afforded a brief period of familiar tranquility, because of all that went with them, the – admittedly brisk – walk through a *quartier* I had once lived in, of which, because it was where I had enjoyed my freedom after leaving Claude, I had fond memories, and then the long pause in the waiting room, a break in the stress of a busy day, it takes me right back to Dr M.'s new, beautifully light consulting room. The light seeped into me, each time I marvelled at it. He was now installed in a street in the Marais, in a former town house, of which the consulting room, with the waiting room, occupied a mezzanine in a narrow building, perpendicular to the main body of the building. There were three walls with windows, so that the light in the room was evenly spread, softened by the fact that the ceiling was very low. As chance would have it, the couch faced the brightest side, overlooking the vast courtyard, which was surrounded on all sides by pale coloured walls, probably because the house had been recently restored. I was reminded of the atmosphere of the little apartment I had lived in years before, in the same street, a few doors up, the first apartment I had ever rented on my own, and which had also had light coming in on three sides. Often, when I left the consulting room, I felt happy, if also rather emotional, and I even looked with some curiosity, tinged with the condescension of the studious pupil, at those who left with long faces, heads bowed, tears in their eyes; I thought I had probably said something which merited further reflection, and I would give it some thought between now and the next session, but, almost as often, I had to admit that the thoughts which had troubled me and the words they had generated did not survive long outside the cosy milieu in which they had originated, and were quickly routed by the joyful animation of the rue des Archives, which led down to the metro station.

Certain reflections, however, have stayed in my mind. One day, when I said that I envied Jacques his ability to immerse himself, by which I implied immerse himself in pleasure – and perhaps as I said this I had in mind the fantasies which always ended with the image of him at the moment of climax, M. asked me to pursue this idea further. I could hardly fail to recognize that I myself was not capable of immersing myself in the strict sense of the word, as I had never learned to swim properly, with my terror of the abyss opening up beneath me as I tried to spread myself in the water. As for immersion in pleasure, I no longer approached this in the same way. I had given up my nocturnal expeditions, during which at one time I would plunge myself into a pleasant state of consenting passivity, in the anonymity of the great body of humanity. My relationship with the moody lover, the one who had played with me as the child in Freud's game of Fort–Da plays with the spinning bobbin, had finally come completely unravelled. For the first time in my life I found myself in a one-on-one sexual relationship with Jacques; the crises did not stop us having sex, even more frequently than before.

Was it a simple one-on-one? Perhaps there was also a third pair of eyes, those of the Observer who took possession of me during my childhood and by whom my consciousness is constantly divided, the intermediary agent of God's omnipresent eye, but also the writer of the script of my life. This is how it worked: the Observer, who in this case took the place of the Dreamer, opened the door of Jacques' world to me, where I took my place in the same way as his other lovers. She welcomed me as though I were a new guest, with no past, no story attached, as though once I was in I could simply let myself go. A new interior, such as a hotel room, where we were staying for the first time, a straightforward meeting in an unfamiliar place, naturally added to my sense of disorientation. But thanks to the peculiar power of the Observer, I was also able to feel it within our own four walls. We had always had a large mirror with a gold frame standing directly on the bedroom floor. Never before had I been so keen to be allowed to stand in front of it, sideways on, naively delighted to observe the ease with which the mechanism of sex made Jacques' member disappear and reappear behind the little hill of my reflected buttock, and the pleasure came from the exact conjunction of feeling his member hitting home inside me and estimating with my eye the point at which it connected to the rest of his body. At other times the Observer would adopt a more social, more conformist point of view, and would take on the gaze of a hotel receptionist welcoming a pair of lovers with kindly complicity, or of the obsequious train employee on the nightsleeper, coming to make up the couchettes.

Or again, she might step aside in favour of the Leica or Sony. Our sexual relationship went through more relaxed periods, which were so welcome after the usual atmosphere of wary tension that we had tended to make the photo sessions which often led into them particularly playful. In my case, they inspired the inner filmmaker in me and set my inner camera whirring. Jacques has always taken photos of me naked, or almost naked, preferably in settings which jarred: car scrapyards, churches, historic sites, out of sight of the guided tour… He strove to make them as incongruous as possible and if, while he was getting ready, I suddenly began to feel the cold, or tore my dress on a twisted car bumper, or a walker or curator disturbed us, I remained unconcerned as long as the lens of the camera was pointed at me. The monstrous monocle fixed to Jacques' eye gave off rays which seemed to clothe me when I was otherwise undressed, and I was completely at ease moving about within its field of vision. When the instruction was to walk towards him, I let myself be picked up by its beam, and while Jacques aimed at me, all I could see was the dark shaft by which I was going to be sucked up, like the genie disappearing back inside the lamp.

During my wandering years I had once had dealings with a man I didn't know, who, all the time he was rummaging away inside me, forbade me to close my eyes. 'Look at me,' he said bossily, almost crossly, 'look into my eyes.' I did my best and perhaps the reason why I have not forgotten this encounter is because the pleasure it gave me was extraordinarily intense. As our eyes met, it created a sort of hyper-awareness of our physical union, and paradoxically set up a distance between us which acted as a kind of crucible of pleasure. I saw him looking at me, and because the facial features are often immobile at the moment when the lower part of the body is most agitated, I could see his expression and his eyes transfixed by this vision, and through him I could see myself in the state which is generally considered more degraded than any other – which of course does not mean that I was passing a judgment on myself or on what we were doing, but that, like all those who, on the contrary, banish morality from their sexual activities, I needed to appeal to it unconsciously in order to get pleasure from transgressing: I saw myself begging desperately for immediate satisfaction. However, I never really appreciated all the twists and turns by which pleasure flows before the change in my relationship with Jacques revealed them to me, and photographic and digital cameras played a large part in my awakening. When our exhibitionist–voyeuristic session leads to coitus, Jacques now likes to flick his eyes back and forth between our bodies, our sexes, and the control screen he holds – which necessarily only shows close-ups – and even if I can't see the image myself, this mediatisation acts as an incredible aphrodisiac. So much so that, even in the absence of any equipment, we recreate the situation. We caress one another, then suddenly I move off, maybe two or three metres from him. With my back turned, I spread my buttocks to expose the flower of the anus and, parting the thicket round the vulva like an image which folds out when you open the pages of a pop-up book, I ask him if he can see everything clearly; implicitly, we work out the distance, which, just for a few moments, is as impenetrable as that imposed by a stage, or a screen; my body is bent, my whole mind is focused on achieving the position I offer him. When it comes to immersion, I like to absorb myself in images. But am I alone in this? Is there, for human beings, any other source of pleasure than that of *obscenity*? Even when two bodies are most closely in contact, do we not take a detour via something beyond this contact, via a projected fantasy or spectacle, even if only in the mind?

So I failed to follow Dr M.'s suggestion. I envied the way Jacques enjoyed his guilt-free sexual paradise. I decided that, by comparison, I had been deluding myself. Ever since the now distant time when, realising for the first time that I was not the only woman Jacques entertained in his bachelor studio, I had fought off my jealousy by boasting, in the letter I'd left him, that I was the most liberated of all women, I had continued to thrive on the idea that sexuality was the field in which I excelled and that, whenever I encountered disappointment or obstacles elsewhere, at least this was an area in which I could feel reassured and flattered, lose myself and soothe my woes, and in which everything would always run smoothly. But maybe my sense of freedom had made me negligent, and in abandoning myself to chance encounters perhaps I had left the possibility of encountering pleasure too much to chance. Perhaps if I had behaved less casually, and not spread myself so thin, I would have been better able to understand what pleasure meant for me, and how to access it. I tried to convince myself with arguments which could have come straight out of a sex manual, and I attributed to Jacques a familiarity with sexual bliss which I myself had been incapable of achieving. During one session I mentioned this conviction in M.'s presence, declaring that Jacques had 'taken over my thing'.

I wasn't much better at analysing dreams, which I always had great difficulty remembering. When I wrote them down and read them back the following morning, they seemed to have nothing to do with me and I quickly became discouraged. On the other hand, I loved wallowing in their atmosphere; even when the atmosphere was oppressive or terrifying, I would prefer not to disturb it with an attempt at interpretation, I would rather remain suspended, like a cloud in a calm landscape. All the same, one day I did turn up at my session with a dream. It has almost faded now, but here is what I still remember. It took place at the psychoanalyst's. He did not open the door to invite me into the consulting room, as he usually did, because this time it was already ajar. The door between the waiting room and his room was situated more or less in the middle, in a kind of alcove or corridor, so that, when, in my dream, I walked through the door, I could see the doctor a little way off, standing in the middle of the room. A woman was standing beside him. That's all. I am not quite sure who the woman was: I don't know whether she was someone I didn't know, or a projection of myself, or a morphing of the two, of the kind that often occurs in dreams. The scene was not sexual, and anyway I have no memory of any gestures or precise words, but it left me with a general feeling of warmth and pleasant ambiguity.

After this dream I remembered a scene, this time a real one, from when I was a teenager. For several years my mother had had this friend who spent a lot of time at our house when my father was absent, sometimes for several days at a time. My brother and I felt we knew him so well we called him Papy. Although we were never told not to, we never spoke of this man in front of my father, which proves that before we could even conceive of the exact nature of his relationship with my mother, we suspected that there was something odd about it, something forbidden, since it had to be secret. But, around the age at which sexuality becomes a more explicit preoccupation, I happened to walk in on Papy and my mother, as they kissed furtively in the doorway of the apartment. I was walking along the corridor which led to the bedrooms and I saw them standing at the far end of the hall, framed in the doorway. My mother had her back to me, but if I close my eyes to try to recall the scene it is her face I see, even so, with that softness to her features, and the expression someone wears when they are calmly, confidently setting about making love. I was shocked but I cannot say exactly why: I doubt whether I thought that their kisses represented a betrayal of my father, since it was already recognized that each of them 'led their own lives', as I had heard it expressed, and I knew full well that my father also had a mistress, or possibly several; I am inclined to think it was a kind of more generalized panic in the face of sexual revelation which comes with puberty, a reaction of extreme modesty, of protection, by an adolescent before she comes under the influence of the thing revealed, a reaction particularly to the sight of her parents, when she discovers that they too, for all their supposed wisdom and authority, are under its sway. If, instead of describing all this in a book, I were to show it in the theatre, the same backdrop could be used for both scenes, that of the dream and of the memory. At the same time as it registers images which enable us to identify faces, objects, landscapes, and unconsciously to establish analogies with others like them, our psyche also registers more abstract structures, spatial layouts which we 'recognize', whatever the decorative detail, the wallpaper of the family home, or the cream walls of the psychoanalyst's room. In other words, just as from day to day we adapt the space around us to our needs and make it serve our own requirements, all of us being, to a greater or lesser extent architects *manqués*, there are also bits of space which resist, the ones which inhabit us, and which in a certain sense imprison us from the inside. I was condemned to the tunnel of the corridor, and to the furtive, but framed vision – of a couple.

M. recommended I read a novel by Marguerite Duras, *The Ravishing of Lol V. Stein*. It was the first time he had ever recommended I read anything! I had never managed to make much headway with the works of Duras, perhaps because, like dreams, they are very enigmatic, requiring the reader to look deep inside herself for the missing pieces of the puzzle, and if I am to be seduced by a piece of fiction I prefer to let it happen more surreptitiously, with less effort. Jacques' comment was that *The Ravishing of Lol V. Stein* was a novel which 'psychoanalysts always found very interesting' . I dived into it; this time, as they say, the spell worked.

We do not necessarily expect the same kinds of pleasure from the various different branches of art, and in my own case, I enjoy entering landscapes and exploring other worlds through reading, whereas I would be more likely to approach people through works of art. It is not surprising that one should wish to identify with sculptures or paintings, our inert but imperishable alter egos, while books, on the other hand, which are fragile but portable, should transport us. The landscapes of Poussin are magnificent but it is the positions of the bodies and the freshness of the faces which touch me; I have never been very keen on Caspar David Friedrich; and my love of the large-scale American abstracts comes from the fact that, in their own way, they are concerned with the body. I would adore to have the right kind of face, and be able to slip into the clothes of the young people in the mannerist portraits, but who could I identify with in *Moby Dick*? Ahab? The narrator? Neither. I can sail off to sea without worrying about either of them much. Is it even possible to be moved by Proust's transparent narrator? Surely Swann is more interesting a character than attractive? Whereas, as the topography of the novel unfolds, one plunges into it like a maze. Even such empathy as I feel for the poignant characters in the works of Bernanos comes as much, if not more, from the damp, muddy atmosphere with which they are imbued, as from their actions, be they saint or sinner.

Then again, when we 'enter' a book, even though it is a three-dimensional object, we move into the fourth dimension of time as soon as we start turning the pages. There is a satisfaction in quickly finding that the portion one holds in one's left hand is thicker, darker with the accumulation of all those printed letters; the darkness of the portion one has read, and which is the past, to which one returns. I am always in a hurry physically to feel the density of this time which is finished, the time of the story, which coincides with my reading time, which is a segment of the time for which I will be alive, time devoted to arranging a space which sometimes transfigures my real environment, and on account of which I will soon begin to regret my haste, because I will find it terribly hard to leave. I never start a book straight after finishing another, I always wait a few days to prepare myself for the change of scene, for the same reasons for which one keeps silent after leaving the cinema; I am crossing a border which requires quarantine.

I could see at once the streets of the town where Lol V. Stein comes and wanders, treading in the steps of a pair of lovers: I assimilated them into the place where the author lived, which was mentioned in the blurb of the paperback edition I bought, the promenade by the beach at Trouville. They also blended with my memories of deserted seaside towns out of season, which for me are always on the Atlantic coast, but this time in Brittany, at Quiberon. The images I have to hand come from my childhood holidays. Because my parents rented a house for three months, our summer holidays were long, and from mid-September onwards, whenever we went down to the beach, the broad residential streets were almost empty, with their huge villas either side, set in gardens whose walls were topped with latticed stonework. Naturally, I aspired to a life which would one day give me access to these villas.

My vision of the scenes where Lol V. Stein hides in the barley field to spy on the couple who appear at a hotel window came from more varied sources. I'm almost sure the famous painting by Andrew Wyeth, *Christina's World*, of the young woman lying in the grass watching the house up on the hill from a distance, must have been one of the models, even though I have never really liked this painter's work. Our unconscious is not always respectful of our tastes. But I needed to fill in the view with some trees because the hotel where the couple is staying is called the *Hotel des Bois*, and also make it night, and the sources for these elements are more commonplace. I think I superimposed images from adverts showing luxury hotels surrounded by high trees, photographed in an idyllic twilight, on illustrations from children's fairy stories in which you see, in the middle of a dense forest, a castle wreathed in a halo of light.

As I made my mental transpositions of these two scenes, I preserved the spare quality suggested by Marguerite Duras' writing. And the care she took in situating her characters in space, each in its exact relationship with the others and with certain landmarks in the scene, a door, a bay window, bus stops, led me to associate them with those small figures you find arbitrarily dotted about architectural drawings and models in active poses, but frozen, a mode of representation I like, because it solidifies the space between the figures and attaches them to their environment. Their suspended gestures make them look as though they are holding space at arm's length; it is as though figures and space were bonded. This bondedness with the world is the same as that of the gullible, defenceless child, who cannot duck a blow aimed at him, nor avert his eyes from a spectacle which entrances him, who has the newborn's ignorance of his own brief past, and does not yet realize that he has an autonomous body, and it felt to me as though the amnesia of Marguerite Duras' heroine, her laconic passivity, were signs of this bondedness. One solution to the coercive nature of our world is to become as mineral as the very things which crush us, to fit in, like a fossil.

The two other protagonists of the novel talk about Lol V. Stein and her solitary walks. They imagine that, by walking, she is 'returning to the past', endlessly recalling the ball where she saw the man she loved leave with another woman and after which she collapsed. 'A depraved woman,' says Tatiana. I underlined 'depraved'. Later in the book, the man, aware that he is being observed by Lol when he meets up with Tatiana at the hotel, pushes his mistress towards the window. 'When she stops, she is perhaps within Lol's field of vision.' And further on: 'She had seen each of us in turn, framed by the window, like a window reflecting nothing, before which she must have had the delicious sense of having been evicted, as she desired.' The two phrases are underlined in the margin. Later on, both of them question Lol: what had she wanted when she saw her fiancé leaving with another woman? Twice over she replied:

'To see them.' Underlined.

I read the book in the Midi, on the terrace, during a period when I was fairly relaxed, and the mere fact of his recommending the book was a concrete sign which boosted my confidence, because I saw it as a suggestion for ongoing conversation which suddenly put me on an equal footing with the analyst, lifting me up, provisionally, from my position down at the level of his knees! It amazes me that the passages I have just quoted, which I had marked with a pencil, did not bring on any sort of illumination. How could they have resonated so clearly with me, without my grasping that they perhaps contained a key which, if I thought about it, would help me understand my suffering, perhaps to assuage it, if not to get rid of it altogether. Admittedly, my small explosions were nothing compared to the deep melancholy of Lol V. Stein, and I had never, gently or otherwise, been abandoned by a man. Even when I was really horrible, Jacques never threatened me with that. After all, if it did ever occur to me to follow him when he had gone to see one of his friends, it was only ever just another fantasy: except in the actual moments of crisis, I retained enough lucidity to steer clear of, without actually really formulating it, the ridicule and real risk which such behaviour would entail, because it was perhaps the one thing which Jacques would not have tolerated. I never actually put it into action. One thought constantly recurred, that I might collect up all the photographs I had found of one of his girlfriends and leave them in a bundle in her letterbox. But this imaginary restitution of her pictures to the model, these reflections of her which I would have gladly clamped down, like a lid on the demon which haunted me, was enough. The pieces of incriminating evidence I found in Jacques' drawer were the only particles of reality I touched, and even then, as I said, it was with the very tips of my fingers.

Most of all, I would not have wished to surprise him in the act because, whereas other men I had been attached to could make love with other women in my presence without my feeling particularly jealous, sometimes just a legitimate little pull on the heartstrings, with Jacques it was quite the reverse, the idea of seeing him doing it is a taboo which I would find very difficult to break. I had come to realize this when the situation arose once, largely at my instigation, right at the start of our relationship, and, contrary to all expectation, in particular my own, I had reacted aggressively. In this there was already a flicker of jealousy, mixed with intuition: the respective places I assigned to each of us from this time on always excluded me from being the one in charge – and I do not believe that, with me, at least, he would have taken the initiative in such a situation. So, although I continued to lead the life of a libertine independently of him, and to claim that sexual freedom was 'my thing', I could no longer do so in his presence, because of the symbolic authority I conceded to him within our relationship.

I spoke very little to Jacques about what I was reading, and I am not even sure I returned to the subject with the man who had recommended it to me. The story of Lol V. Stein spoke to me vividly, but at first I did nothing with it, I kept it up my sleeve. In fact, I did not interpret it fully until much later, when I wrote my book on Salvador Dalí, where there is much discussion of voyeurism and the feeling of banishment. Have you ever felt tempted, for example, after a particularly tiring experience, such as a physically demanding journey, to put off

as long as possible the moment of well deserved rest, to avoid
rushing into immediately enjoying having got where you
wanted, choosing rather to wait, or, while you are at it, to
make one last effort, to tidy the room before going to bed,
summon up your strength to climb just a few metres more for
an even better view, really just so as to experience one last time
the masochistic sensation of your pain-numbed muscles, pro-
longing it before the promised relief? I did not immediately
manage to shake off my paralysis. Whenever I had read
psychoanalytical works, I had been amazed by how obvious
the solution to the cases discussed turned out to be; the person
with the problem gave a more or less detailed account of his
childhood memories and his dreams; he always remembered
them with a clarity I found enviable; thanks to some slip of
the tongue, or detail in a dream, the origin of his mania or
inhibition or phobia popped up like a bad genie from the box
of his unconscious. Eureka! A decisive clue enabled him to put
his finger on the origin of his plot against himself in one single
leap. I did not have a brilliant denouement of this kind, I just
started to feel a bit better, the crises came less frequently, and
one day it occurred to me that I had not come into analysis to
talk about my little worries at the office.

Dr M. had now moved, and instead of setting out my
memories and my feelings like fruits spread out to dry in the
dappled sunshine, and watching them take on the warm
colours of their surroundings, I was now talking in a mezzanine office which received no daylight apart from through a
bull's eye window onto the waiting room, which was very
dark. You came in through a door under the main entrance to
the building, which must once have been a concierge's lodge
and in which the only light came in through a glass door,

which was admittedly quite wide, but led out into the courtyard. Part of this narrow waiting room was under the mezzanine, and therefore in an alcove, which heightened the feeling
of oppression. When I came in I had no sense that my morbid
thoughts would turn into light, airborne particles, I felt I was
more likely to slide into a state of gloom. I had begun to write
The Sexual Life of Catherine M. As soon as I received the contract from the publisher, I announced it gaily during a session,
while they were still being held in the brightly lit room. Now
my sessions were increasingly spent discussing whether or not
I should end the analysis… Each time, the doctor would walk
as far as the door with me, saying 'See you on Thursday', or
'See you next week'. Finally, one day, I shook my head and said
no, giving as my reason that I needed time, 'time to write this
book'. I galloped down the narrow stairway between the consulting room and the waiting room. It would be true to say
that I made good my escape.

on the beach

I was a very young art critic when a publisher commissioned me to write a history of modern art. It was towards the end of the seventies, and modern and contemporary art did not attract the same audience as they do today. Not much had been published on the subject up till then, and they were placing considerable trust in me by giving me such a huge project. I was self-taught, and was at the stage where for my own education I was methodically visiting all the museums. I immediately set to work: futurism, expressionism, constructivism, Dadaism, Bauhaus and De Stijl… I read everything I could get my hands on, filled notebooks with hundreds of quotations which might be useful, and consulted early printed sources which were just catalogues containing, at best, poor quality black and white reproductions printed on cheap paper that dulled the images. I must have written two or three chapters, mostly during the summer holidays, which we spent in Florence. I wrote in stifling heat, at a minuscule table installed under some large trees, at the far end of the garden of a villa near the Porta Romana, part of the basement of which we had rented. But once we returned home I became too caught up with practical problems at *Art Press*, and uncertainty over its future, to carry on with it regularly. I neglected the work, which in any case required more maturity than I had then. The editor who had given it to me left the publishing house and no one ever asked me to produce anything. I held on to the idea that if I should ever publish a book, it would be a kind of broad survey. I had failed, on this occasion, to fulfil my ambition, but it did not go away. At that time my conception of art history, in common with many of my artist friends and colleagues, was teleological; the way to tell a part of this history would have been to explain why I thought certain contemporary works were good, but the demonstration had to be comprehensive if it was to be irrefutable. There was also the fact that my idea of what a book was was linked to the way I worked. In contrast with my daily activities, where anything could happen, a book was a rare and necessary object; you only had to write one book, so long as it was something like a masterwork in the original sense, except that instead of being a qualifying piece for the practice of a craft, it was the culmination of it, condensing all the experience and knowledge which had been acquired. My aborted essay taught me to be more realistic about my abilities and to be prepared to wait. I did not have to wait long. Five or six years later a different editor asked me to write an overview of contemporary art in France. It was a more sensible project. It gave me the chance to treat the subject according to my ideal, as exhaustively as possible, and I submitted a large manuscript.

I am aware that my conception of books is similar to my conception of love! Although I am a libertine, I have definitely never been flighty. I consider people who have one love affair after the other as though they were members of an alien race, whose language and customs are mysteries to me. I am hopelessly, discouragingly sceptical about those romantic souls who succumb to love at first sight. My own experience is so different! It took many years, thousands of conversations, a few shared tribulations, until, without of course having thought it through, I identified the feeling I had for Jacques as a feeling of love. Even then it was a little while before I told him. We had just moved into our new house. In the evenings, once the light was off, I lay thinking. There would be a moment of silence, marking a divide with the rest of the day and then I would ritually decide to wish him good night, sometimes adding 'I love you'.

Continuing my dedication to works of synthesis I later wrote a book which covered the whole of the international contemporary art scene, for a reference list which, again, required me to do a roundup of the subject. Once this work was finished, I found myself for the first time in my professional life with no big job on hand. I was available, and the idea of writing *The Sexual Life of Catherine M.* suddenly came to me. Originally, it was one of those rather frivolous thoughts which enable us, from time to time, to detach ourselves from daily existence when it becomes disagreeable or boring. We plan to do something later, in some hypothetical future in which we will be fulfilled or grown up but whatever it is remains vague. We never bother to clarify it. It could easily just be one more hazy idea among many, which throughout the rest of our lives would occasionally make fleeting reappearances, keeping alive, until time begins to run out, the possibility of a different life. But here I was, seriously intending to do it: write an autobiography which would only take into account my sex life. (To be honest, 'seriously' is rather too strong a word, since I could only envisage the project dimly, without immediately being able to distinguish it clearly from fantasy.)

Now I am writing a new autobiographical book, for which I actually had the idea very soon after the publication of the first book, as a necessary extension to it, which I had not previously thought of. I am aware of the various precautions I have taken: the frequency with which I use expressions like 'it seems to me', 'I think I remember', the use of the conditional. As an obsessive, I find honesty requires me to indicate when my memory or analytical sense fail me, and when I find myself resorting to supposition, while making every effort, of course, to be scrupulous. But lapses of memory are all part of one's autobiographical material, and I make no attempt to hide them. In Picasso's sculptures, after all, there is as much left out as there is filled in, and perhaps memoirs should also take into account, to some extent, the things we have forgotten. Thus I am quite sure that I first had the idea for a book called *The Sexual Life of Catherine M.* before the crisis described in these pages, but I find it difficult to put a date on it. Or to say when I first mentioned it to anyone else. Sometimes I question the people around me in an attempt to prompt my own memory, but when I asked Jacques he couldn't remember either. I am quite sure that it crystallised during the crisis.

The idea came back to me during the course of a conversation with a friend, who later became the book's publisher, who was telling us how he wished he could find some novels or stories by women talking about their attitudes towards sexuality. Jacques encouraged me: 'You should do that book...' I hear myself saying: 'Yes, yes... the books I've written so far have done all right...' I spoke of the book as though it was another book on art. Though I still didn't know what I was going to put in it, exactly, nor how I would set about it, I felt fairly confident. I didn't have that feeling of joy you get when you have the chance to realize a long-cherished project or ambition. At the very most, I felt light-hearted at the thought of the bizarre nature of the undertaking. I felt as I had at twenty, when it seemed to go without saying that the art world would welcome me with open arms, simply because that had always been my dream. My reply to Jacques was a conventional one, but this was not an attempt to strengthen my resolve, but rather to curb what might otherwise look like cockiness.

One thing did worry me though: the question of what used to be called 'style', and which now would probably be called 'writing'. Because a large part of my culture came from the avant-garde, and this is where the contemporary works which interested me took their references from, I had it in my head that a piece of writing which had no journalistic or didactic function must necessarily find a new form of expression. Like those painters I admired who had reinvented everything from scratch, starting with nothing but a width of raw canvas, I thought I needed to find a totally new way of putting the words in order. I have always kept the poems I had shown the young maths teacher when I was fifteen or sixteen in cardboard boxes. He had returned them to me with annotations as though he had been correcting an exercise in prose composition. He criticized the innovative layout I had come up with, with line breaks and indentations, sometimes in the middle of a phrase. 'Still the same problem with layout!' he had written in the margin. He had also paid me several compliments. I had shown him a short story, which was unfinished, about a woman with no name, wandering about an unknown, deserted town. She entered a dark, mysterious house. There, another woman, 'well-built, and dressed in a straight black dress' took her by the hand and led her over to a group. My mentor had written 'TB' in connection with a phrase I will copy out here: 'Men dressed mostly in soft beige and grey were tossing playing cards, dusty and yellow with age, onto baroque café tables, their attitudes so oddly brusque as to look like plain indifference'. He had even underlined, 'soft beige and grey'. The taste of my first reader had been contaminated by the same classical style which I used for my characters' dress, and from this I drew the conclusion that what had appealed to him was the classical evocation and form. The descriptive phrase, rather than the unexpected caesuras. Later on I showed these poems, and others I had written since, to Claude. He found them pretty, but meaningless. I never showed them to Jacques because he was a writer and with him I would have been ashamed of these puerile first attempts.

I had signed the contract for *The Sexual Life* with no hesitation, but since I was unable, for reasons to do with work, to start immediately, I spent several weeks puzzling over it, as disconcerted as I had been thirty years previously. I basically thought the subject required me to invent a formula, like a cook who has some unusual ingredients and must make up some new recipes. But how, and out of what, should I develop mine?

The solution was given to me one spring afternoon, between the sand and the sky. We had come for a walk on a beach which we often chose on days when the wind was high; because it partly runs along the foot of a cliff, it is protected. That day it was deserted, and because it was not yet warm, the air was clearer than in summer. I find conversation during walks most useful, because being out in the open disinhibits my mind. Thought is like a cupboard which, from time to

time, in the true sense of the word, needs airing. I consider the
view, I gaze at the empty horizon or, immediately in front of
me, the tips of my shoes on the bumpy pathway. I do not see
the person I am talking to, I merely sense his presence, the
more so because it is my point of anchor in the landscape. I
can escape the gaze which might judge me, aware only of his
reassuring proximity. Just at that moment we were having a
rest. I was sitting on the sand and while I talked I was making
an imprint of one of my hands. Behind me was the cliff, which,
for several years, I had not climbed. The path leading up, the
flat plateau at the top, in which the only features were a light-
house and some bushes, had once also been part of our walk.
But I no longer wanted to go there, since reading among
Jacques' papers that he had at various points along the way had
sex with a girlfriend, which I had found humiliating because it
is a very open spot and for this reason, whenever I had been
accompanying him, we had always decided against it. Had he
been more daring with her than with me because he had
desired her so much? If we returned to these giddy heights
together, the memories they brought back, which I could not
share, would cast me out for sure.

This time, I had forgotten about it, because, for better or
worse, there is nothing more absorbing than questions of technique. They can easily become obsessive and in this case, they
drove out all other thoughts, including the most corrosive. I
was listening to Jacques, who was walking up and down in
front of me. When I looked up at him I could not really make
out his features against the light, but his gestures as he accentuated his point were silhouetted clearly. He explained that I

needn't worry, I should set about this book in the same way as the others, with my usual clarity and precision. It was a subtle relief. We formed a single point of shade, and as the light flooded towards us, a convergence occurred: I received Jacques' words trustingly, the solution he was proposing was already within me, my past life would find its way into a book, the advice he was giving me for this book would be the start of a new life for me.

I began making notes shortly after that, very systematically. On the first page I drew up a list of all the names I knew of men with whom I had had a physical relationship: I could remember them all. Then, because I am first and foremost extremely receptive to sensations connected to spaces, I immediately, and quite naturally, allowed space to dictate the thematic divisions of the book. I classified my memories according to these themes, without imposing a hierarchy. Once I had put my memory in order, I began writing.

The worst of the crisis was over, but I still had relapses. It is remarkable that these upsets had no effect on the progress of my work. A discussion might have degenerated into a row the previous evening, I might have spent part of the night sobbing, but I still set serenely about my work the following day, describing a scene in a swingers' club or some erotic ritual Jacques and I had been engaged in. I was so absorbed by what I was writing that none of the usual day-to-day upsets had any impact. Perhaps these upsets already belonged to the past, whereas the memories I was recalling, paradoxically, were part of my present. When I had almost finished writing the book I even realized something. Before I started it, I had occasionally planned to slip in some mean little remark, never directly addressed at Jacques, always at the women: a detail about their lives or their physique which I knew, and which might have annoyed or humiliated them if they recognized themselves. But no, my story never led me to include this sort of detail.

My attention was focused solely on the female protagonist of this story, written in the imperfect, the tense of estrangement and closure. I discovered that as one's dreams of the future gradually become fewer, because one no longer has sufficient future left for them to be full and varied, memories come to take their place. I have not given up those long periods of mental perambulation, but I explore fewer prospective paths. I measure my advancing years not by the lines on my face or the stiffening of my limbs, but by the curtailing and impoverishment of my ability to dream. A necessity and a gift: time passes, and, happily, certain expectations one had early on in life have one way or another been met. But despite this I rarely formulate new ones. I understand Rousseau's melancholy: 'My dimmed imagination no longer flares up at the sight of the beloved object, I am less intoxicated by wild dreams; there is more reminiscence than creativity in what it produces these days.'

To daydream about something is not a rational project, and it is not possible to measure the length of time – short or long, now or later – it will take. Time in daydreams is like time in Utopia, indeterminate, a notion which our psychology can scarcely render, except by a word like 'distant', and even before the weakening of our body reduces the space within which we operate, the space in which our imagination is active has already lost that vagueness of horizon which means it can be taken over like a virgin country.

The distance we set between ourselves and the events of our past life, which reduces their scale, the backlog of things we failed to notice at the time, the logic which connects them, which back then was invisible, the light shed on them by the epoch they belong to, which mankind already considers a moribund piece of history, their ultimate strangeness, which makes us look back on the person we were as though they were a different being, all these things conspire to turn our past into a dream. It is said that the future narrows once we cease to believe that it is eternal, but the troubled curtain of emotion and feeling is raised to reveal regions of the past which we were unaware of, and this is what seems to open up now. We become the reader of a novel of which we were once the unconscious author, and before embarking on the final chapter, the skilful author may hand us a key which suddenly allows us to link together all the clues scattered through the story, giving meaning where once there appeared to be none. In this way, we can use the pleasure which comes from recognizing a hidden meaning to stave off sadness, regrets or nostalgia, the anguish of arriving at the final chapter.

When I was young, I often dreamed about my future, but always with such confidence in life itself that I never sought to bring reality into line with my utopia. I was proud, I let fate decide. As a moralist, I have always mistrusted those who lead their life as though it were a novel which they first worked out in their heads, 'who make up the story of their lives'. On the other hand, I now know that each person, if he is prepared to look back, can discover that his past truly is a novel, and that however full of painful episodes it may be, this discovery is a joy.

The scene with my mother embracing her lover in the doorway of the family apartment had brought the following comment from Dr M.: 'What saved you was seeing your mother in the arms of another man.' A more perceptive reader than myself, more experienced in the workings of the unconscious, will perhaps be able to make sense of this phrase, at least to base some sort of supposition on it. Once again, I was unable to make much of it, too many of the clues which might have helped me understand it were still hidden from my understanding. But perhaps it was sufficient that I knew I was 'saved', without knowing exactly from what, nor why this vision had been able to do the saving. Since I was not able to interpret it, I accepted the remark without triumphalism, indeed, without conviction, taking it simply as a generally favourable sign. The vision of my mother served as the opening to a paragraph in this book, in which I otherwise placed myself at the centre of almost every scene. I began to be less haunted by the visions of Jacques in the company of other women.

I am still troubled if I hear someone speak the name of one of these women, and sometimes I take the initiative myself, to test my immunity, or rather to check that I am *not* yet completely immune. Every now and then, I find myself unfolding a crumpled piece of paper Jacques has left lying around – a pure reflex action.